The Great Little Book
Of Fun Things
You Probably Don't Know
About Ireland

Unusual facts, quotes, news items, proverbs
and more about the Irish world, old and new

2nd Edition

By Robert Sullivan

ISBN: 1-4392-5254-8
Copyright 2013-2014 Rum Point Digital, Inc.
P.O. Box 1773
Port Washington, NY 11050
publisher@irishletter.com

Dedicated to:

Mary Dooney Sullivan
County Roscommon

Jeremiah Sullivan
County Kerry

Contents

Introduction

The tiny nation of Ireland has always had a cultural "vibe" that seems to reach out and touch the entire world. While Americans, in particular, seem to accept this as quite normal, writers in Ireland have long questioned why everyone around the globe finds them so darned interesting.

The Cliffs of Moher on Ireland's Western Coast

Of course, the fact that the Irish often can't see what's so unique and wonderful about their country is a big part of their charm. In my own 30 years of visiting Ireland and dealing in various capacities with the Irish, I've learned that, under the surface, they're more complex than they seem at first blush.

As much as any visitor, I appreciate their almost unbelievable warmth toward strangers. But I also know that, in spite of the easy banter and joking, getting an Irishman to express his real feelings about something can be the toughest thing on earth.

Under the surface of Ireland, there's a world of ideas and customs that's sometimes brilliant and often a bit nutty. I got interested in collecting facts about Ireland many years ago, and I've found that, no matter how many layers of Irish culture you peel back, there always seems to be another one beneath.

This list of Irish facts comes from all sorts of places - from my Irish Nana (grandmother) who told me they used to call a young pig a "bonnif" in Roscommon where she grew up, to facts from Irish books, newspapers and websites I've looked through over the years. I can't absolutely guarantee the accuracy of each fact here, but I've made an effort to use trustworthy sources. If you see something incorrect or have an interesting fact to suggest for the book, feel free to email me at *publisher@irishletter.com*

I hope you enjoy this survey of Irish culture, both old and new.

Robert Sullivan

1 Eccentric Irish Traditions

A single day of good weather that pops up in a long stretch of bad days is traditionally known in Ireland as a **"pet day."**

Couples in Ireland could marry legally on St. Brigid's Day (February 1st) in Teltown, County Meath, as recently as the 1920's by simply walking towards each other. If the marriage failed, **they could "divorce" by walking away** from each other at the same spot, on St. Brigid's day the following year. The custom was a holdover from old Irish Brehon laws, which allowed temporary marriage contracts.

Ancient Brehon Laws, which governed Ireland from Celtic times up to the 17th century when they were supplanted by English law, gave **an extraordinary level of power and independence to women**. They were allowed to hold government office and marry or divorce a man according to their wishes. They actually had a legal right to experience "satisfaction" in marriage, though the meaning of that provision was a bit vague. Women were allowed to inherit property, and could receive a husband's property in a divorce if he was deemed to be the cause. Amazingly, Brehon laws also recognized the concept of copyright. In the year 561, one monk (Finnen) sued another (Colmcille) for copying a version of the Latin Bible he had illustrated. A regional king ruled in favor of the plaintiff, stating rather stylishly "To every cow her young cow, that is, her calf, and to every book its transcript. And therefore to Finnen belongeth the book thou hast written, O Colmcille."

All windmills in Ireland turn in a clockwise direction, while the rest of the windmills in the world turn counter-clockwise.

According to legend, the devil spat out **the Rock of Cashel** while fleeing Ireland after its conversion to Christianity by Saint Patrick.

According to tradition, a wedding party should always **take the longest road home from church.**

Some of Ireland's most bizarre ancient superstitions:
- Shaving every Sunday causes toothaches.
- Cutting a baby's fingernails before he turns one year old will make him a kleptomaniac.
- Crossing a stream of running water at night will keep evil spirits from following you.
- Locks of hair must be hidden from birds. If a bird finds a lock of your hair and brings it to a nest, you will suffer from headaches.

Dublin was originally called "Dubh Linn," which means "Black Pool." The name refers to an ancient treacle lake in the city that's now part of a penguin enclosure at the Dublin Zoo.

Ireland's first saint was not Saint Patrick. He was **Saint Abban**, who went to preach in England during the 2nd century.

Handfasting is an ancient Celtic custom, once practiced in Ireland and Scotland, where a bride and groom came together at the start of their marriage. Their hands (their wrists, actually) were literally tied together. The term "tying the knot" as a description of getting married traces to this custom.

The Newgrange passage tomb in County Meath was constructed around 3200 BC, making it more than 600 years older than the Giza Pyramids in Egypt, and 1,000 years older than Stonehenge.

Aran Island sweaters have a variety of **"family weaves."** These were developed because when a fisherman drowned, his sweater would often be the only thing washed up on shore. The distinctive weave told a family their loved one had been lost.

St. Patrick introduced the Roman alphabet and Latin literature into Ireland. After his death, **Irish monasteries became Europe's leading intellectual centers**.

Traditionally, Irish wakes are held in private homes and not in funeral parlors.

In the days of sailing ships, Irish sea captains often carried **pebbles from Scattery Island**, the home of the Saint Cannera, the patron saint of sailors.

The Vikings founded Dublin in 988.

The **last witch in Ireland** was supposedly Dame Alice Kytler, born in Kilkenny in 1280. All four of her husbands died, and she was accused of poisoning them. Today you can dine at Kytler's Inn in Kilkenny, which operates in her old home.

Irish tradition says that finding a four leaved clover brings you luck, as long as you find it accidentally. The first leaf is believed to represent faith, the second hope, the third love, while the fourth leaf represents luck. About one four-leaf clover occurs naturally for every 10,000 three-leaved clovers. The scarcity, however, seems to only encourage collectors. According to *Wikipedia*, one collector has amassed over 160,000 four-leafers.

The first three days of April are called the "Borrowed Days" and are traditionally associated with bad weather. This derives from an old legend about a mythical cow who boasted that March was unable to kill her. March borrowed three days of terrible weather from April to try to finish the cow off for good.

Irish Child Naming Patterns:
In case you're wondering which relative to name your kids after, here are the traditional naming patterns from old Ireland:
1st son: Named after father's father / 1st daughter after mother's mother
2nd son: named after mother's father / 2nd daughter after father's mother
3rd son: named after the father / 3rd daughter after the mother
4th son: named after father's eldest brother / 4th daughter after mother's eldest sister

An old legend says that, while Christ will judge all nations on judgment day, **St. Patrick will be the judge of the Irish**.

A small number of devotees still go to holy wells in Ireland to **"pay rounds,"** by circling a well three times and making a sign of the cross over it with a pebble. All ceremonies at holy wells were once frowned upon by The Church, which saw them as holdovers from Ireland's pagan era.

The term **"Emerald Isle"** first appeared in a poem called "Erin," written in 1795 by William Drennan.

In the 17th century, a command to **"Hang the harpers wherever found"** was given by Queen Elizabeth, who wanted to extinguish all aspects of Irish culture.

I'll just take the hangover, thanks: One traditional Irish cure for a hangover was to be buried up to the neck in moist river sand.

Saint Patrick's tipple. It was once popular in Ireland to pin sprigs of shamrocks on your coat on Saint Patrick's Day in remembrance of his using shamrock leaves to illustrate the idea of the holy trinity. At the end of the day, one would **"drown the shamrock"** by putting a few shamrocks into a glass and covering them with whiskey.

"Cemetery Sunday" is a lesser-known tradition still practiced around Ireland, although it seems to take place on whatever date is most convenient for local church leaders. A mass is celebrated with families of those buried in the local church graveyard, after which an effort is made over several days to clean up the churchyard. The congregation also tends to graves of those who have no one left among the living to remember them.

A **jaunting car** is a traditional Irish horse-drawn vehicle with two wheels, which can carry four passengers and is driven by a man called a "jarvey."

The traditional **Irish Easter "cake dance,"** in which the best competitor wins a cake, is called a "pruthog."

An odd Irish birthday tradition is to **lift the birthday child upside down and give his head a few gentle bumps on the floor** for good luck. The number of bumps should allegedly equal the child's age plus one.

The word **quiz** was allegedly invented in the 1830's by a Dublin theater owner named Richard Daly, who **made a bet that he**

could make a nonsense word known throughout the city in just 48 hours. Legend says that Daly gave his employees cards with the word "quiz" written on them, and told them to write it on walls all over the city. Some historians argue that the word was already in use at this time, but most agree that it did not acquire its current definition – "to question or interrogate" – until sometime in the 19th century.

Montgomery Street in Dublin was **once the largest red light district in all of Europe**, with over 1600 prostitutes plying their trade. An old Irish song called "Take Me Up To The Monto" memorializes this era.

The national symbol of Ireland is the **Celtic harp**, not the shamrock.

In olden days, a pig was often allowed to live in the house with the family on an Irish farm. He (or she) was commonly referred to as **"the gentleman who pays the rent."**

Medieval laws in Ireland allowed a man to divorce his wife if she damaged his honor through infidelity, thieving or **"making a mess of everything."**

Doctor John Osborne of Dublin had himself buried in an **upright coffin** when he passed away in 1864. The good doctor wanted to be sure he could stand out and be counted on resurrection day, in spite of his arthritic hips.

For two hundred years, an ancient oak tree in County Down produced a ringing sound every time the wind blew, leading to stories of faeries and ghosts. In 1885, the tree fell down in a wind storm and a gold bell came tumbling out of the trunk – a relic apparently planted by monks many years earlier.

Until recent times, Irish farmers called a young pig a **"bonnif,"** a term also used by farmers in Newfoundland.

"11th Night" is a celebration still widely observed by Protestant groups in Northern Ireland, who build huge bonfires across the country on the night of July 11th. The fires are lit on the night before the July 12th commemoration of William of Orange's defeat of King James, a Catholic, in 1690 in the Battle of the Boyne. The battle took place near Drogheda, north of Dublin.

A particularly quirky old belief in Ireland is that it is a **bad luck omen if a chair collapses** after your rise from it.

In rural Irish townships, **so many families have the same name that a curious form of identification has been used over the years**. A person's first name is combined with the first name of his or her father. So Maggie Sullivan, for example, is called Maggie Jerry, with Jerry being her father's name. As a result, people know which local Sullivan family she comes from. (On a visit to Ireland in 1999, the author of this book spoke with a local parish priest who said that in the religion class he taught at a local school, 18 out of the 23 students were named Sullivan!)

2 Lesser-Known Irish Facts

The original Guinness Brewery in Dublin has a **9,000 year lease** on its property, at a perpetual rate of 45 Irish pounds per year.

The longest place name in Ireland is **Muckanaghederdauhaulia**, in County Galway.

The first Irish Constitution was signed at Dublin's Shelbourne Hotel. The Shelbourne, a favorite spot for sophisticated travelers to stay or dine, re-opened in 2008 after a major facelift.

Ballygally Castle in County Antrim, currently a hotel owned by a major chain, is allegedly **one of the most haunted places** in the country. Lady Isobel Shaw, whose husband built the castle in 1625, is said to knock on doors at night and then disappear. While alive, Ms. Shaw was locked in her room by her husband and starved, until she leapt to her death from a window.

The island of Montserrat is sometimes called **"The Emerald Isle of the Caribbean,"** and has a shamrock carved above the door of the governor's home, areas called Cork and Kinsale, and people with names like O'Garra and Riley. This is because the island was originally settled in 1633 by Irish-Catholics, who came from the nearby island of St. Kitts. (After a major volcanic eruption from 1995 - 2003, Montserrat is now partially open to tourism again.)

According to some historians, **over 40% of all American presidents have had some Irish ancestry**.

The very last ship built by **Harland and Wolff** in Belfast, famed for constructing the Titanic, was a ferry called the Anvil Point, launched in 2003.

The "Oscar" statuette handed out at the Academy Awards was designed by **Cedric Gibbons, who was born in Dublin in**

1823. Gibbons emigrated to the US, and was considered MGM's top set designer from the twenties right on through the fifties, working on over 1,500 films. After designing the coveted prize, Mr. Gibbons managed to win a dozen of them himself.

Famous wit Oscar Wilde was born **Oscar Fingal O'Flahertie Wills Wilde** in Dublin in 1854. Wilde died penniless in Paris, France, in 1900.

Bram Stoker was working as a civil servant in Dublin when he wrote "Dracula" in 1897.

Berkeley, California is named after George Berkeley, who was the Bishop of Cloyne in County Cork from 1734 to 1753. **Bishop Berkeley's world views would have been quite at home in California**. He founded a school of thought called "Immaterialism," which taught that there is no material substance in the world, and that the only reality is "that with can be perceived by the mind." Hence, "to be is to be perceived." Immaterialism has also come to be known, perhaps satirically, as "subjective idealism."

The lyrics to "Danny Boy" were allegedly written by an English barrister named Fred Weatherly, while he was riding on a commuter train.

Dubliners jokingly refer to the massive statue of Wolfe Tone that stands in St. Stephen's Green as **"Tonehenge."**

In 1859, **Irish scientist John Tyndall was the first to correctly explain why the sky is blue**. The explanation may surprise you. The sun puts out a full spectrum of light colors – but your eyes are most sensitive to blue and red/purple colors. Molecules in the air scatter the sun's blue light faster than they scatter its red light. A day-time sky without clouds looks blue because the sun is close to you, and relatively little of the blue light has been scattered. You see red and orange colors at sunset because the light must travel a greater distance to you, and all the blue light has been refracted away from your line of sight by the time the sun's light hits you – not because of dust or other particles in the air as is widely believed.

The very first St. Patrick's Day parade in America was hosted by the Charitable Irish Society of Boston in 1737.

Historians believe **St. Patrick's real name** was "Maewyn Succat."

"Gulliver's Travels" writer Jonathan Swift is **buried in St. Patrick's Cathedral in Dublin**

"The Taking of Christ" by Caravaggio, which hangs in the National Gallery in Dublin, was **"lost" for 60 years – hanging anonymously in a Jesuit monastery.** It was recognized in 1990 by an art expert when it was brought in for cleaning. The painting, valued at over $30 million US, is on "indefinite loan" to the gallery from the Jesuits.

In 1942, Belfast was the first place in Europe visited by an **American troop ship** en route to the battlefields of World War II.

Tory Island, about nine miles off the coast of Donegal, is frequently unreachable by ferry in the winter months due to high seas (it has no airport, though a small helicopter visits it twice a week from November to March). In the 1970's, **the Irish government attempted to move its entire population to public housing on the mainland, so the island could be used as an artillery range**. But the fiercely independent islanders, who elect their own "King of Tory" to watch out for their interests, refused to leave. Today the island has about 200 residents, including a widely known colony of artists.

The rocky region in County Clare known as "The Burren" is one of few **"karst"** areas (a limestone area covered with caves, fissures and underground streams), so named for a similar area in Slovenia. The Burren is famous for its explosion of wildflowers in springtime.

Tarzan's first Jane in the movies was **Maureen O'Sullivan, who was born in Boyle, County Roscommon in 1911. She played the part of Jane six times** opposite Johnny Weissmuller, ending with "Tarzan's New York Adventure" in 1942, and appeared in over 65 other movies, including

"A Day At The Races" with the Marx Brothers. Edgar Rice Burroughs, who wrote the Tarzan books, called her the "perfect Jane." She died in Arizona in 1998.

The tune of the **"Star Spangled Banner" was composed by the great blind harper Turlough O'Carolan**, who died about 35 years before the American Revolution.

Some historians say that the world's **first execution by guillotine occurred in 1307** in County Wexford.

Temple Bar district in Dublin got its name from **Sir William Temple**, whose home and gardens were located there in the 17th century ("bar" happens to be a common Anglo-Saxon name for a gatehouse).

Achill Island is the largest island off Ireland's coast. It's 56 miles square, with dramatic landscape featuring wild cliffs and moors.

Killary Bay, on the Mayo-Galway border, is **the only true fjord in Ireland**. A fjord is a long, narrow inlet from the sea between high slopes.

Director John Huston filmed the New Bedford, Massachusetts scenes in his 1956 movie **"Moby Dick" in Youghal, County Cork**.

Fastnet Rock, about four and a half miles off Cape Clear Island and Mizen Head in Ireland's southwest corner, was long known as the **"teardrop of Ireland."** That's because it was the last piece of the country seen by emigrants sailing to America from Cobh, the most popular point of embarkation for those abandoning the Emerald Isle.

Famed **Hollywood movie director John Ford** was born Sean O'Feeney in 1894, in Spiddal, County Galway.

"The Rotunda" hospital in Dublin, founded in 1745, is **the oldest hospital specializing in maternity in the world.**

The Liffey Bridge in Dublin is also known as the **Ha'penny Bridge**.

The oldest golf club in Ireland is the Royal Belfast. Founded in 1881 in Kinnegar, Holywood (County Down), it was later moved to nearby Craigavad. The current course was built in 1926, and has changed little since. Among the things characterized as "unacceptable dress" for members playing on it are denim of any kind, combat pants and "garments displaying excessive branding."

Louth is the **smallest county in Ireland**; Cork is the largest.

About 30% of the people in Australia are of Irish descent.

Actor Kenneth Branagh hails from Belfast.

Bushmills, in County Antrim, Northern Ireland, is **the oldest distillery on the island**. It was first licensed in 1608.

The O'Connell Bridge in Dublin was originally built with rope. **Only a single man and a donkey could cross at once**. It was replaced with a wooden bridge in 1801.

Ireland's highest mountain is Carrantouhill, in County Kerry (3,445 feet).

It **rains about twice as much in The West** of Ireland as it does in The East. Clouds that come in off the Atlantic, heavy with moisture, tend to release as they hit the coast.

James Gamble, a co-founder of Proctor and Gamble, was born in 1802 in Enniskillen in Northern Ireland. In 1819 he emigrated with his family to America, where he attended Kenyon College. In 1837 he founded Proctor and Gamble with William Proctor, a brother in law. James Jr., one of his ten children, was a chemist who created the formula for Ivory soap.

Because the Lusitania sank so quickly after it was torpedoed off Old Head of Kinsale in 1915, **only 6 of the ship's 48 lifeboats ever made it to nearby Queenstown** (now known as Cobh).

Shannon Airport is on **NASA's list of emergency landing sites for the space shuttle**.

Over 100 **bottlenose dolphins** live in the Shannon Estuary, on Ireland's west coast between the Kerry Head and Loop Head peninsulas.

There are towns called **Dublin** in California, Georgia, Indiana, Maryland, New Hampshire, Ohio, Pennsylvania, Virginia and Texas.

In 1941, **Belfast was bombed** several times by German aircraft. On one night, over 900 people were killed.

The Republic of Ireland is about the same size as **West Virginia**.

The Irish-American rock group "Black 47" is named for **1847**, considered the very worst year of the potato famine in Ireland.

During World War II, **Hitler seriously considered invading Ireland**, to use it as a platform for an assault on Britain. At the same time, the British repeatedly pressured Irish Taoiseach Eamon De Valera to give them use of the ports of Cobh, Berehaven and Lough Swilly for ships involved in their anti-submarine campaign in the Atlantic. De Valera refused, citing Ireland's neutrality in the war.

Between 40 and 44 million Americans (about 13% of the population) claim some Irish ancestry, making them the **second largest ethnic group** in the US. People of German descent are the largest group.

The first **submarine** in America's military was built by John Philip Holland, who emigrated to America from County Clare. Holland built his prototype, called the *Holland VI*, in Elizabeth, NJ, and tested it in New Suffolk, on eastern Long Island, in 1899. The US Navy purchased it from him on April 11, 1900.

Ireland's total full-time defense corps, including all army, navy and air corps personnel, numbers less than 14,000 people. All enlistment is voluntary.

At upscale Longueville House in Mallow, County Cork, 2,000 pheasants are brought onto the grounds each year for

the pleasure of hunters. They arrive in late summer and are kept well fed and protected from predators, and are then released in January. In addition to live prey, hunters can elect to take part in "simulated clay shoots," where, according to the resort's website, "An array of different quarry will be simulated from coveys of partridge, eye squinting high pheasants and duck to looping pigeons and curling woodcock. At the end of the last drive the guns return to the cozy bar."

Carnlough's (County Antrim) Londonderry Arms Hotel recently celebrated its **one hundred sixtieth anniversary**.

An Taisce (ann taska), Ireland's largest environmental advocacy group, has rated Dublin as not only **"the dirtiest major city not just in Ireland, but in all of Europe."**

The Brazen Head, located near the Guinness Brewery in Dublin, is said to be the oldest pub in all of Ireland, founded in 1198. It's not clear how much of the original building is still there. The historical-feeling spot has, over the years, served a pint to revolutionaries Robert

Emmet and Wolfe Tone, as well as James Joyce, Jonathan Swift, Michael Collins, Van Morrison and yes, even Garth Brooks. In addition to music, the pub hosts regular storytelling sessions (though Sean's Bar in Athlone, founded some 900 years ago, and Grace Neill's Bar in Donaghadee also claim to be the nation's oldest watering holes).

According to Ireland's Central Statistics Office, car ownership in The Republic reached an all time high in 2006, **with one private car existing for every two adults in the nation**.

In the 16th and 17th centuries, Belfast was the unquestioned world capital for making linen. The design and manufacturing skills for linen were brought to the city by Huguenots fleeing religious persecution in France.

The only American president not born in the United States was Andrew Jackson. He was born on a ship in the Atlantic Ocean in 1767, which his parents were taking to the U.S. from Carigfergus in County Antrim.

Some historians believe that **distilling was first done in Ireland and not Scotland,** as is widely believed. Missionary monks who came to Ireland as early as the 7th century apparently distilled a fruit or grape brandy, primarily for medicinal purposes. The first whiskey made from a barley base was apparently distilled in Ireland in the 1500's.

At the Jameson Distillery in Midelton, County Cork, thousands of bottles worth of whiskey evaporate each year from the oak casks where it is placed for maturing. This lost portion is known as **"the angel's share."**

The very **first Irish parliament** met in College Green, Dublin, in 1264.

During the 1916 Easter Rising, **hostilities were halted twice each day to allow for the ducks in St. Stephen's Green to be fed**.

Ireland's Saint Fiacre, born in the sixth century, is the **patron saint of gardeners**.

The River Bann in County Wexford is a **hot spot for eels**. Every spring, over twenty million of them show up there to breed.

The original seven "Celtic Nations" are: Ireland, Scotland, Wales, Isle of Man, Cornwall, Brittany (in France) and Galicia (in Spain).

Kilkenny-born architect James Hoban designed the original White House in Washington after winning a competition sponsored by President George Washington and Secretary of State Thomas Jefferson in 1792. It's said that Jefferson submitted his own design under a pseudonym but failed to take top prize. When the White House was burned by the British during the war of 1812, Hoban was called in to oversee a three-year-long restoration of the building.

Ernest Shackleton, famed for his participation in the **1901-1904 Antarctic** expedition across the Ross Ice Shelf, was born in Kilkee, County Clare.

The first American general to die in The Revolution was Richard Montgomery, who was born in Donegal.

The northern Spanish town of Santiago de Compostela is known as **"el Dingle de Santiago"** in memory of a journey that Irish religious pilgrims made there in medieval times.

The **red kite**, an almost extinct species, was reintroduced in County Wicklow Ireland in the fall of 2007. The red kite is a raptor that has been supported by special breeding and release programs in England. It has not been seen in Ireland since the 19th century.

Pop singer **Christina Aguilera's** mother is Irish-American.

President Barack Obama's maternal great, great, great grandfather Fulmuth Kearney came from Moneygall, County Offaly. Mr. Kearney arrived in the U.S. in 1850. When Obama visited Ireland in May, 2011 to a tumultuous welcome, he told a Dublin crowd of over 25,000 "My name is Barack Obama, of the Moneygall Obamas, and I've come home to find the apostrophe we lost somewhere along the way."

Belleek Pottery, located in Belleek, County Fermanagh (Northern Ireland), celebrated it's 150th birthday in 2007 by reissuing 15 items from deep within its design archives, including a 19th century Round Tower centerpiece. All pieces in the "Archive Collection," which range in price from about $100. to $400., are individually numbered, and available in limited quantities.

Trinity College in Dublin, which happens to be Ireland's oldest university, has famous alumni including **Oscar Wilde and Bram Stoker.**

Limerick was sacked so many times in the 17th century it was once known as the "city of sieges." In more recent history it has had so many gang killings it's become known as "stab city."

In spite of a recent baby boom and the return of many emigrants, Ireland's population **is still not as large today as it** was in **1841, at the outset of the potato famine**.

The lives of Ireland's Travellers (yes, that's with two l's), formerly known to many as "tinkers," have always been difficult. The traditionally itinerant people have long been subjects of suspicion and derision by the broad Irish population, and it's been documented that they suffer high unemployment rates and exceptionally short life spans. Nonetheless, the number of Travellers in Ireland has risen from 20,000 in 2007 to over 36,000 in 2012, according to Pavee Point, an advocacy group. But being a Traveller doesn't necessarily mean being on the road these days. Just 12% of the Travellers now live in caravans or motor homes. The vast majority, who define themselves as an ethnic group rather than simply as itinerants, live in private or government sponsored housing. The painted horse wagons associated with them, which were still very much in evidence through the 1970's, have completely vanished from Irish roads.

41

Sales of Guinness Stout have been falling in recent years, **but Irish whiskey is hot,** hot, hot. Sales of whiskey from the old sod jumped 130% between 1994 and 2005, according to the Distilled Spirits Council of the United States.

In a recent national survey conducted for Catholic and Protestant organizations, only 5 per cent of Irish 15 to 24-year-olds could quote the first commandment. About one-third didn't know where Jesus was born, and amazingly, 35 per cent said they **did not even know what is being celebrated on Easter**.

Interest in **Irish-speaking schools** has exploded in Ireland in recent years. Almost 65 "Gaelschoils" have opened in the last decade, and many have long waiting lists of students wanting to get in.

One of Ireland's stranger political episodes was the **"Independent Soviet Republic of Limerick,"** formed on April 15, 1919, in the midst of the Irish War of Independence. It was created as a response to British army's declaration of a "special military area" covering Limerick City and part of County Limerick, which in turn was a response to a general strike organized by the Limerick Trades and Labour Council. The Limerick Soviet printed its own money, and gained considerable media attention in Europe and The United States. But when the strike ended on April 27th the Soviet was dissolved, just two weeks after its founding.

Former British Prime Minister **Tony Blair's** mother was born in Ballyshannon, County Donegal.

Killyleagh Castle, in County Down, Northern Ireland, is **the oldest occupied castle in Ireland**. Built in the 13th century, it is still in use as a private home.

The Irish tricolor flag, created in 1848, was designed to **reflect the country's political realities**. Orange stands for Irish Protestants, green for Irish Catholics and the white stripe for the hope that peace might eventually be reached between them.

Thomas Blood of County Meath was the only person who was ever crazy enough to try and steal England's crown jewels. Just to add to the degree of difficulty, Mr. Blood attempted his heist in broad daylight on May 9th, 1671. Oddly enough, instead of having him hanged, King Charles II pardoned Blood and actually gave him a large financial award because he was so impressed by his bravado.

The **"man engine"** is a tower on the hills high above Allihies, near the end of the Beara Peninsula in County Cork. It was erected in 1862 to lower workers mechanically into the copper mines in the hills. It's the only such structure in Ireland on one of few in the world. Allihies was a major center for copper mining in the 19th century.

In 1800, **the population of Ireland was almost twice as large as that of the United States**. By 2000, America's population was about 60 times that of Ireland.

St. Patrick had a very limited education, and is said to have been **self-conscious about his weak writing skills**.

Catherine Kelly, who died in 1785, was allegedly **the smallest Irish woman ever**. With a total height of just 34 inches and a weight of 8 pounds, she was known as "The Irish Fairy."

Ireland was **once densely forested,** but was practically denuded of tree cover in the 17th century.

Grace O'Malley, known as the "**Queen of the Pirates**," commanded a ship with a crew of over 200 men off the west coast of Ireland in the 1500's.

The oldest traffic light in Dublin stands in Contarf, next to the original home of Fergus Mitchell, **the first person to ever own a car in Ireland**. Installed in 1893, the light still works.

3 Modern Marvels

In 2011, Irish milliner Philip Treacy gained attention by **designing 35 different hats worn by ladies at the wedding of Kate Middleton and Prince William** in London. Treacy hails from a rural village in County Galway.

So long paddy wacker. Wooden truncheons, which have been carried by Irish gardai (police) since the 1800s, were finally phased out in 2006 and replaced by lightweight retractable batons. The truncheons, with notches, fancy carvings and names cut into them, were often passed down through generations of gardai.

County Mayo's Carne Golf Links, which was built between 1987 and 1993, was **constructed mainly by farmers using hand spades and rakes**.

Playboy Magazine was banned until 1995 in Ireland, though the magazine's TV channel was available well before then.

According to *Forbes Magazine*, **five Irish citizens are billionaires**. The wealthiest of all is 83 year old Pallonji Mistry, who became a citizen through marriage to an Irish national, but who lives in Mumbai, India. Forbes says there are about 1,400 billionaires worldwide.

The Irish Academy of Engineers has recommended that **a tunnel be built under the sea linking Ireland and Wales**. The IAE has offered a futuristic vision of trains running at speeds of 150 mph between Rosslare and Fishguard, Wales. Currently, there is no financial backer for the project.

One of the most popular radio shows in rural Ireland is still the weekly **broadcast of local obituaries**.

Ireland's 15 main railway stations are **named after the leaders of the 1916 uprising**.

An "An Fáinne" is a lapel pin, worn by some fluent Irish speakers **to invite others to speak to them** in the traditional language.

The scenic "Wicklow Way" is the oldest and most popular hiking route in Ireland. Stretching from the Dublin suburb of Rathfarnham southwest toward the village of Clonegal, in County Carlow, the 25 year-old public walking route is traversed by **over 20,000 people each year**.

Britain is actually the world's #1 market for Guinness. **Nigeria is #2**, out ranking and out drinking Ireland itself, which ranks #3.

In the early 20th century, The Abbey and Gate Theaters in Dublin mounted plays by Synge, Shaw, Yeats, O'Casey and others that were so scandalous that people took to calling the two venues **"Sodom and Begorrah."**

Even before the economic pullback of 2008, the Vintner's Associate of Ireland reported **that rural pubs were closing at a rate of one every day**, due to the combination of rising costs, the then-new ban on smoking and tougher laws against driving under the influence. Now, it's reported that bar sales have fallen by almost a third since then, and the total number of pubs in the country has fallen from almost 10,000 to about 7,500. Two culprits that have accelerated the fall of Irish pubs are the growth of alcoholic beverage sales in supermarkets and the rising taste for wine, which Irish people tend to drink at home more than in pubs.

Owen Nolan is **the only Irish-born player to have ever played in The National Hockey League**. Nolan, whose middle name is Liam, was born in Belfast. He was selected number one in the 1990 NHL draft, and played for seven different NHL teams before retiring in 2012. The power forward never won the Stanley Cup, but he won the Olympic gold medal (playing for Canada) in 2002 and played in five NHL All-Star Games.

Ireland has virtually **no coal deposits, even though it's just 60 miles from Wales**, one of the world's richest coal fields.

Muhammad Ali has some Irish heritage.
His great grandfather was born in Ennis,
County Clare, and emigrated to Kentucky in
the 1860s. There, he married an African-
American woman. A son born to this couple
also married and African-American woman,
who gave birth to Ali's mother, Odessa
Grady. She married a man named Cassius
Clay, and the two moved to Louisville, where
the future champ was born.

Baileys Irish Cream, which was launched
in Ireland in the early seventies, is now the
most popular liqueur in the world.

It's **not the custom in Ireland to wear
green ties,** hats or other green clothes on
St. Patrick's Day. A sprig of shamrock in the
coat lapel is the preferred display.

In 1999 an ad was published in an Irish
magazine called "Buy and Sell." It read:
"**Gravestone, £250**. Would suit someone
with the name Burns."

One old Irish superstition holds that **May is
an unlucky month to get married in,**
because of its association with the Virgin

Mary. This superstition seems to have lost its power, however, since May is now one of the most popular wedding months for Irish people.

The Irish tricolor flag, created in 1848, was designed to **reflect the country's political realities**. Orange stands for Irish Protestants, green for Irish Catholics and the white stripe for the hope that peace might eventually be reached between them.

Although the influence of the Catholic Church has faded considerably in Ireland, one of its orders is flourishing. **Dominican Friars, who live in 16 different priories across the country, have seen a surge of new young men wanting to join in recent years**, according to *The New York Times*. One key reason is the bad economy, which has made even successful young professionals consider the idea of pursuing a more spiritual life. Another draw of the Dominicans is the fact that they still wear the traditional monk's habit, an 800 year-old garment consisting of a white tunic and black capuce. These medieval-looking robes help distinguish the monks clearly from parish priests, who wear the traditional black and white collars. That has turned out to be a good thing for the monks in an era of Church scandals. Dominicans elsewhere in the world are also seeing an upsurge in new vocations.

Irish (it's officially "uncool" to call it gaelic now) is the third most widely spoken language in Ireland, according to the 2011 census. **Ahead of it, in the number two slot, is Polish.** Yes, Polish. A huge influx of Eastern Europeans, driven by Ireland's entry into the EU (which allows citizens to move freely among member nations) has resulted in about 119,000 people speaking Polish at home in Ireland, versus 82,000 speaking Irish outside of school, where it is a required subject at the secondary level. A far larger number of people, about 40% of the population, say they are able to speak Irish but don't. English, obviously, is the leading tongue.

Ireland is the ninth most **oil-dependent economy** in the world.

Bertie Ahern was sometimes called the **"Teflon Taoiseach"** after surviving a political scandal in 2006, when loans he received from friends when he was finance minister in the 1990's came under scrutiny.

Henry McCullough, the lead guitarist in Joe Cocker's band, was **the only Irishman who played at the original Woodstock music festival**.

There are currently **no nuclear power plants** in The Republic of Ireland or in Northern Ireland.

Bernadette Devlin, born in County Tyrone, was elected as a representative of Northern Ireland in the Westminster Parliament in 1969 at the age of 21. **She is still the youngest women ever to have been elected to the British Parliament**.

Except for special detachments, **Irish police do not carry guns**.

Dublin is the #1 European destination for so-called **"stag" or "hen" parties put on before weddings** by visitors from the

United Kingdom. Irish news writers frequently mention that drunken English women in hen parties are a problem in the Temple Bar District.

A popular online guidebook, *The Lonely Planet Bluelist*, has named **Northern Ireland as one of the world's "must see" destinations**.

American pharmaceuticals are big business in Ireland, and that has become a problem due to changes in the pharma business. After exporting over 11 billion Euro worth of life sciences products to the U.S. in 2011, mostly from factories owned by Pfizer and other American companies situated "offshore" in Ireland, exports plummeted by almost a third during 2011 - 2012. The fall was caused by rising price competition among drugs in the U.S., and the expiration of patents on many big-selling medications. It's a staggering blow to Ireland, which depends on drug shipments to The United States for 50% of its manufacturing export sales.

The Irish Times reports that **Emily** and **Jack** are currently the most popular names being given to newborn Irish children. Seán, Daniel and Conor are the next most widely given boy's names, while Emma, Lilly and Grace are in fashion for girls.

So long Irish siesta. Hour and a half lunch breaks, long a staple in laid-back Ireland, are fading fast as the economy booms. *The Irish Post* reports that about half of all Irish workers say they're now too busy to leave the workplace for lunch even once a week.

Knock, in County Mayo, is a world famous Catholic shrine often visited by religious pilgrims. But a crowd of more than 10,000 less reverent types showed up there recently after a self-proclaimed visionary announced a precise moment when the Virgin Mary would be appearing there. **He provided a DHA or "definite hour of arrival" (unlike the ETA or "estimated time of apparition" other wacko mystics have named in previous years)** and hired a public relations agency to spread his message. The group that came to see the big moment included more punk rock girls in high heels and miniskirts than pious worshipers, according to Knock's manager, who complained to *The Irish Times* than many also had "spray-on tans."

An Irish bride's family was once expected to foot the bill for the entire wedding (and often hand over some farming land to the groom as well). No more. Nowadays couples are seeking financial help from both sets of parents to put on the happy event.

About 5.6 million pints of Guinness are consumed worldwide on an average day. **On St. Patrick's Day, that number rises to 13 million pints**.

"Gazumphing" is a term widely used to describe a shady practice that was popular at the height of Ireland's real estate boom. It described a tactic where real estate agents accepted a bid from one buyer, and then accepted a higher one even as contracts for the first bid were being processed. The agents would then go back to the first bidder and demand more money to match the new, higher bid. In Ireland, there is normally a period of several months between a bid being accepted and a closing taking place. "Gazumph" is a Yiddish word meaning "to swindle." The term is now fading into history, due to the near-total collapse of Ireland's real estate market since 2008.

The Irish Stock Market (ISEQ) lost almost 80% of its value from 2007 to 2009. Since then, it's recovered about only about 20% of that loss, in spite of seeing economic growth of 4.7% per year, more than twice that of the United States. Continuing hard times in the financial sector are a big drag. Many of Ireland's top banks, including AIB and Bank of Ireland, lost 99% of their value during the crash, and have never risen back up beyond the level of penny stocks.

Since the start of the Iraq war in 2003, American soldiers have made over two million stopovers at Shannon Airport on their way to and from the combat zone, with up to three military flights calling there each day. U.S. military use of the airport is controversial in Ireland – some rights groups claim that CIA "rendition" planes are also using the airport. According to the

Move To Ireland newsletter, the American government pays 7 million Euro each year for use of the airport.

2012 saw the release of a documentary made by Peter Whitehead (in a recently re-edited version) about a 1965 tour of Ireland by the Rolling Stones. Entitled **"Charlie Is My Darling,"** in honor of the group's drummer, it is actually the first professionally filmed footage taken of a performance by the band. The brief tour of Belfast, Dublin and Cork City had the Stones, clad in conservative jackets and button down shirts, being virtually attacked onstage by rabid fans. According to bassist Bill Wyman, Irish fans constantly sought "contact, any sort of physical contact…just to say they touched you."

The issue of drinking and driving in Ireland has gone through some curious permutations in the past decade or so. In 2005, a series of tough new laws were passed to increase testing and get more drunk drivers off the roads. The result: the number of drunk drivers reported in Ireland jumped 23% in the first half of 2006 over the previous year. But by the end of 2012, drinking and driving seemed to be in rapid decline, with about 9,000 arrests occurring in the year, versus 19,000 drunk driving arrests in 2007. *The Irish Times* reported that a key reason is a "cultural shift," in which the Irish have come to take a more negative view of getting behind the wheel while intoxicated. There's not a complete lack of sympathy, however, for blotto drivers. **In 2011, the County Kerry Council passed a law allowing people in rural areas to drive while under the influence of alcohol.** The law was designed to "prevent loneliness and reduce the risk of suicides among those who live in Ireland's backcountry."

Irish police (gardai) have received increased government funding to battle a **rising problem of armed gangs trading in drugs and stolen cars**. The cities most affected have been Dublin, Sligo, and Limerick, and there have been problems in counties Clare, Tipperary and Cork.

According to a 2007 Bank of Ireland report, **Ireland was the second wealthiest nation**

in the world, with over 30,000 millionaires. By 2011, The Bank of Ireland seemed less inclined to issue any report on world wealth, and the International Monetary Fund rated Ireland as the world's 14th wealthiest country.

Because of population shifts towards big towns and cities, some parts of the countryside are increasingly populated only by old folks. **Over one-third of the population in some Irish rural areas is now over 65 years of age**.

The first divorce ever granted by the Irish government was in 1997.

An Irish jig (usually "The Irish Washerwoman") was played for many years in Detroit's Joe Louis Arena each time **Brendan Shanahan** scored for the Red Wings, as it was in Madison Square Garden when he played for the New York Rangers until his retirement in 2008.

Ireland is **not a member of NATO,** but has been a member of the European Community since 1973.

Ole! **About ten percent of County Roscommon's population is Brazilian today**. The samba is danced in local clubs on "Brazil Nights" and one local radio station broadcasts in Portuguese on weekends.

"Trocaire" is a widespread practice of charity during the Lent season in Ireland. It's hard to call it a tradition, since it was only started in 1973 by Irish Catholic Bishops. But it's certainly popular. In 2007, over 10 million Euros were collected by children who brought small cardboard "Trocaire boxes" home to stuff with their parents' extra cash. The proceeds go to foreign development offices of The Church, with about 60% being dedicated to Africa.

There are more cell phones than people in Ireland, according to CIA World Facts. Oddly, Ireland's average of 102 phones for every 100 people is lower than the European Union average of 107 phones per 100 people.

Ireland is currently the world's second largest exporter of software, according to Enterprise Ireland. That's partly because it's well located to be a major shipping point, not just to all of Europe but to the Middle East as well, for Microsoft, IBM and other big American tech companies.

11,000 people ran in the 2012 Dublin marathon. About half were foreigners.

Real estate prices in Ireland rose over 150% from 1997 to 2007, the largest increase for any European country. Property values have plummeted about 50% since then, though they still remain almost double what they were in 1997. Whether a bottom has been reached or not is questionable. In 2012, housing values fell once more - by about 4%.

Youth movement. Ireland currently has the highest proportion of people under 25 of any member-state of the European Union.

Ireland has the **second highest number of lawyers** per capita in the world – after the United States.

The human hardships of Ireland's famine in the mid 1800's are well known. But less often discussed are the effects that it had on Ireland's long term population picture. According to an analysis of census figures by *The Irish Times*, if the famine had not triggered a massive population decline in Ireland through emigration and other factors and **Ireland had followed the typical demographic pattern of other European countries since 1841, there would now be 17 million people living in the Republic,** rather than the current 4.6 million population.

Ireland is the **most "globalized" country in the world,** according to a recent study by A.T. Kearney and *Foreign Policy* magazine. The country's high volume of trade with other nations and "personal contact" with people internationally (many of whom are connected to Ireland by family ties) were two key factors in gaining the #1 rating.

Brick-throwing among teenagers living in mixed Protestant and Catholic areas in Northern Ireland is still so common - and so pointless - that authorities sometimes refer to it as **"recreational rioting."**

The Irish Examiner announced in 2007 that Irish workers are, on average, **losing up to seven years of sleep** over their lifetimes because of the time they spend driving to and from work. The three most sleep-deprived professions: 1) doctors, 2) company directors and 3) train drivers. Decide for yourself whether sleep-deprived doctors or train-drivers scare you more.

Ireland's top star in the sport of hurling is Sean Og O'Hailpin, who was born to an Irish father and Fijian mother on the tiny island of Rotuma, an isolated atoll about 400 miles north of Fiji. O'Hailpin, whose very Pacific appearance is a bit of an anomaly in Irish sports, has been declared "Hurler of the Year" and "Sports Personality of the Year" by RTE. He plays for the Cork County team.

Late Show host David Letterman once described the uilleann pipes as **"a sofa cushion hooked up to a stick."**

Possibly the strangest event in Ireland is "Tedfest," an annual gathering of fans on Inis Mór (Inishmore Island, in Galway

Bay) that honors, in a manner of speaking, "Father Ted," an oddball but highly acclaimed show that ran on Irish TV from 1995 to 1998. Set in a fictional location called Craggy Island off Ireland's west coast that seems similar to Inish Mór, the show followed the misadventures of two Catholic priests surrounded by a decidedly wacky group of islanders. Every February, about 300 Ted fans now arrive on Inish Mór dressed as nuns, priests and bishops and spend three days doing nothing more than drinking, singing songs from the show and generally acting silly. Most locals, who were originally unsure what to make of the Ted fans, seem to have now embraced the festival as a rare boost for mid-winter tourism for their island. On attendee, quoted in the Irish Times, said "If you're not cracked, you may as well not come. The minute you get off the boat and put your foot on the ground, you turn into a lunatic."

The Irish lumper, the species of potato that figured heavily in the Great Famine, is about to return after a 170 year absence from the island. Introduced to Ireland in the early 19th century, the lumper became wildly popular because of its high nutritional value and its ability to grow in even the worst soil. Unfortunately, by the 1840's Ireland had become so dependent on it that when it was quickly wiped out by a blight, a cataclysmic famine resulted. Antrim farmer Michael McKillop has now re-cultivated the lumper, making it available to the Irish for the first time since the pre-famine era. In spite of a reputation for tasting "awful," he says the classic spud is quite tasty.

An unemployed artist has chosen to lodge a unique protest against Ireland's adoption of the Euro currency, which he feels is a major cause of his country's economic downturn. Frank Buckley has built an apartment within the lobby of a new Dublin office building that has sat vacant since its completion a few years ago. **The apartment is built from the shredded remains of 1.4 billion Euros,** obtained from the Irish national mint. Mr. Buckley says a bank gave him over 350,000 Euro during the boom to buy a home, even though he had no real income. Now, having lost the home and his wife as well, he is living in his protest structure and adding on a kitchen and other rooms.

Police in Dublin, one of Europe's most traffic-congested cities, have been trying control illegal parking by clamping "boots" onto the tires of violators. Each year, more than 60,000 illegal parkers are getting the boot along with a fine of €80. **Unfortunately, it costs almost €160. to get a boot onto each car when the total costs of the program are added up.** The City of Dublin is now losing about €5 million each year on the enforcement program.

4 Irish Christmas Facts

Christmas whitewashing: Around Christmastime, you'll still find the odd farm building out in the Irish countryside that looks like it's just been whitewashed. Long ago, farm families cleaned and then whitewashed every building on the farm in December. They were covered in white paint or limewash, to symbolically purify them for the coming of the savior. The tradition traces back thousands of years, not just through Celtic culture, but through other Central European cultures as well.

The Gaelic way of saying "Merry Christmas" is "Nollaig Shona Duit." It's pronounced "null-ig hun-a dit."

Some historians believe the song **"The Twelve Days of Christmas"** originated in 16th century Ireland and England. It was supposedly designed to help young Christians remember Church teachings, at a time when Catholicism was strictly outlawed in both countries. The "partridge in a pear tree" represents Jesus, the "two turtle doves" represent the old and new testaments, and the twelve days are the days between Christmas and the Epiphany. Some argue, however, that the song originated in France.

Before Christmas trees: Having an evergreen-type Christmas tree is a relatively new phenomenon in Ireland. Years ago, whole families went out to find holly bushes and ivy to decorate the mantelpiece and other parts of the house. Finding a holly bush with lots of berries was considered a harbinger of good luck in the coming year. Holly was also used because it allowed poor people to decorate their homes in the same way as those who were better off. The bush was so common in Ireland in winter that there was plenty for everyone.

"Little Women's Christmas," on January 6th, is a traditional day for Irish women to leave their housework behind and go out with each other to have fun. It's a very old holiday, kept alive today by a few enthusiastic Irish ladies.

It's considered **bad luck to take down holiday decorations** before "Little Women's Christmas" (sometimes simply called "Little Christmas") on January 6th.

A welcoming candle: A Christmas candle in the window is still popular in Ireland. Historically, window candles were a symbol that the homeowner would welcome the Holy Family – unlike the inn keeper in Bethlehem who bore the guilt of having turned them away. **During times of intolerance for Catholicism in Ireland, window candles also were meant to announce that it was safe to say Catholic mass in a home**.

Leaving a mince pie and a bottle of Guinness out on Christmas Eve was once popular in Ireland. It was meant to be a snack for Santa Claus.

Ancient Celts believed mistletoe had tremendous healing powers. Christians considered it such a strong symbol of paganism, in fact, that they banned it until the so-called "revival of Christmas" in the Victorian era.

On December 8th, **the Feast of the Immaculate Conception, virtually all schools in Ireland are closed**.

Pantomimes are still performed by small groups of amateurs and professional actors alike in the days following Christmas. Irish "pantos" are humorous productions of Cinderella, Snow White and other familiar fairytales. In them, men frequently play the part of women and vice versa. Generally, there's a great deal of singing and dancing, with jokes making fun of eminent politicians or celebrities thrown in.

Children in Ireland are accustomed to finding presents left by Santa in their bedrooms, often in a sack at the foot of the bed. An occasional big gift may be left under the Christmas tree, but it's usually unwrapped.

The Irish Christmas Tree Growers Association, which has a goal of fostering the production of "real" Christmas trees in Ireland, has about 100 members. Those of us who've virtually never seen a tree in Ireland are interested to know that the Christmas tree group is actually an outgrowth of the Irish Timber Growers Association (ITGA).

Christmas' Roman origin? "Saturnalia," a Roman feast dedicated to the god Saturn, was celebrated on December 17th in pre-Christian times. Some historians believe the holiday was adopted by Christians throughout Europe in the fourth century, and turned into a commemoration of Christ's birth. The date was changed to December 25th to coincide with the winter solstice on the Roman or "Julian" calendar. Other old pagan holidays were "Christianized" (All Hallows day for example), because the Church wanted to adopt holidays people were already celebrating widely. A Roman practice of cutting down an evergreen tree on Saturnalia may be the origin of the modern day Christmas tree.

5 Irish Words & Meanings

"Keening" is the Irish version of loud crying at wakes practiced in several European cultures (Italy, in particular). It involves wailing and expressing endearments in Gaelic to the deceased. **At some wakes, the Keening once went on for hours, with many participants**.

"Slan," which is used widely in Ireland to mean "farewell" or "until we meet again," translates to "safe" or "keep safe" in old Irish.

"Erin go Bragh" means simply **"Ireland forever"** in Irish.

A **"planxty"** is a song composed for a specific patron.

Celtic rockers the Pogues were originally called "Pogue Mahone," which means "kiss my a**" in Gaelic.

There are seven huge stone forts on the Aran Islands: Dun Aonghasa, Dun Ducathair, Dun Eoghanachta and Dun Eochla on Inishmore; Dun Chonchuir and Dun Fearbhai on Inishmaan, and Dun Formna on Inisheer. **The preface "Dun" means "fort of a chieftain."**

"Hibernia" is the name ancient Romans called Ireland. It may come from the word "hibernus," which simply translates as "wintry." Some, however, say it comes from "Ivernia," a Latin version of "Erin," Ireland's mythological name. The Romans never managed to make Ireland a part of their empire.

"The Snug" is a small private room in older, traditional Irish pubs, often favored by ladies.

"Sean-Nos" is a highly ornamental style of a capella (no instrumental accompaniment) singing that came mainly from the west

Galway region, and which is still practiced by many Celtic singers today. Sean Nos translates, literally, into "old style."

The Phrase "by hook or by crook"
allegedly comes from a military campaign by English bad guy Oliver Cromwell, who in 1649 planned to attack Waterford by taking ships around Hook Head or marching through the village of Crooke. Some say Richard DeClare, Earl of Pembroke first used the expression to describe Cromwell's invasion. Cromwell failed, while DeClare succeeded in capturing Waterford.

"Tallaght" in Dublin is an old name that means "**The Plague Cemetery**."

Though it's only one of many theories, there are those who believe the term "**put the kabash**" on something comes from an old Irish phrase "cie bais," which means "cap of death."

The term **"painting the town red"** derives from the story of the Marquis of Waterford, who in 1837 allegedly rode through a town in England with a group of drunken friends slapping red paint on all the buildings. Back home in Ireland, the Marquis was known as a "reprobate and landowner" (according to the Oxford Dictionary of National Biography), who was known for fighting, stealing, painting the heels of a horse with aniseed and hunting the animal with bloodhounds. As a young student, the Marquis was "invited" to leave Oxford University.

Irish castles and round houses often have a lobby inside the front door called a **"murder hole,"** with an opening in the ceiling that defenders could use to shoot at or pour hot liquids onto unwanted guests.

Ross Castle, a 15th century structure in Killarney National Park in County Kerry, has at its core a spiral staircase built in a clockwise direction to force attackers to hold their swords in their left hands or be interfered with by the central structure if they used their right hands. **It also had stairs of uneven height, to throw off the gait of any attacker**.

The term "hillbilly" was first used in America to describe the immigrants from

Northern Ireland, mostly Presbyterian, who came in the 18th century. The name had been attached to them back in Ireland since the 1600's, when southern Irish Catholics started calling Protestant supporters of King William "hillbillys" or "billy boys."

"Fianna Fail," the name of Ireland's ruling party, means **"Soldiers of Destiny"** in English.

"English follows the roads" (*leanann an Bearla an tearr*) was a popular expression in Ireland's rural west during the early 1800's. It referred to the large-scale building of new roads (and whole towns) in the countryside, which brought more English-speaking people to areas where only Irish language had been spoken previously.

"Beyond the pale," an expression used to describe outrageous behavior, originated in Ireland in the 14th century. The Pale was the area of Ireland under heavy British control. People living in areas outside it were considered wild and outlandish.

A **"Slane"** is a long, slim blade used for cutting turf.

"Black Irish" people, who have black hair and swarthy skin, are thought to descend from sailors of the Spanish Armada, who came ashore when their ships were wrecked off Spanish Point (County Clare) in 1588.

The word **"slogan"** comes from the Irish *sluagh-ghairm*, which means "war cry."

The ball used in the game of hurling is called a **sliothar** (*slit-or*). The stick that players carry is called a "hurl," or "hurley." The wide part at the top of the stick is called the "boss."

The common prefixes of "Mac" and "O" in Irish family names translate, respectively, into "son of..." and "grandson of..." in Gaelic.

The word **"galore"** comes from the Irish *go leor*, which means "enough" or "plenty."

6 Irish Proverbs

"Nil aon tintean mar do thintean fein."
There's no fireside like your own fireside.

Man is incomplete until he marries. After that, he is finished.

A silent mouth is melodious.

Three things come without asking: fear, jealousy, and love.

It is sweet to drink, but bitter to pay for.

Idleness is a fool's desire.

"Coimhéad fearg fhear na foighde."
Beware of the anger of a patient man.

A diplomat must always think twice before he says nothing.

A lie travels further than the truth.

Marriages are all happy. It's having breakfast together that causes all the trouble.

Better to be a coward for a minute than dead for the rest of your life.

If you want an audience start a fight.

A man loves his sweetheart the most, his wife the best, but his mother the longest.

A scholars ink lasts longer than a martyr's blood.

Don't break your shin on a stool that is not in your way.

If you dig a grave for others, you might fall into it yourself.

A poem ought to be well made at first, for there is many a one to spoil it afterwards.

The Irish forgive their great men when they are safely buried.

A change of work is as good as a rest.

A good retreat is better than a bad stand.

"Ní bhíonn airgead amadáin i bhfad ina phóca."
A fool's money is not long in his pocket.

"Ní thagann ciall roimh aois."
Sense does not come before age.

"Níor bhris focal maith fiacail riamh."
A good word never broke a tooth.

Drink is the curse of the land. It makes you fight with your neighbor. It makes you shoot at your landlord and it makes you miss him.

A spender gets the property of the hoarder.

"Is maith an t-anlann an t-ocras."
Hunger is the best sauce.

"Is minic a bhris beal duine a shron."
It's often a person's mouth breaks his nose.

Put a beggar on a horse and he'll ride it to hell.

"Is beo duine gan a chairde ach ni beo duine gan a phiopa."
One may live without one's friends, but not without one's pipe.

Never tell secrets to your relatives' children.

Cheerfulness is a sign of wisdom.

"Maireann croi eadrom i bhfad."
A merry heart lives long.

"Dafheabhas e an t-ol is e an tart a dheireadh."
Good as drink is, it ends in thirst.

You've got to do your own growing, no matter how tall your father was.

Both your friend and your enemy think you will never die.

It's not a delay to stop and sharpen the scythe.

Only the rich can afford compassion.

There's many a ship lost within sight of the harbor.

The dog that's always on the go is better than one that's always curled up.

Listen to the sound of the river and you will get a trout.

It is a long road that has no turning.

An ounce of breeding is worth a pound of feeding.
- Horse racing expression meaning that thoroughbreds are born and not made.

The day will come when the cow will have use for her tail.

May you live as long as you want, and never want as long as you live.

Necessity knows no law.

Every patient is a doctor after his cure.

There's no forcing the sea.

Trouble hates nothing as much as a smile.

There is no virtue in the herb that is not got in time.

7 Unusual Irish Quotations

"A drunkard is a dead man, and all dead men are drunk."
- Yeats

"Every action of our lives touches on some chord that will vibrate in eternity."
- Sean O'Casey

"Everywhere I go I'm asked if I think the university stifles writers. My opinion is that they don't stifle enough of them. There's many a best-seller that could have been prevented by a good teacher."
- Flannery O'Connor

"I spent 90% of my money on woman and drink. The rest I wasted."
- Soccer superstar George Best

"We have always found the Irish a bit odd. They refuse to be English."
- *Winston Churchill*

"If you're thinking about your eyebrows while you're acting, you're not acting properly."
- *Milo O'Shea, actor known as "the Irishman with the eyebrows"*

"The conclusion of your syllogism, I said lightly, is fallacious, being based upon licensed premises."
- *Flann O'Brien*

"All the world's a stage and most of us are desperately unrehearsed."
- *Sean O'Casey*

"My favorite optimist was an American who jumped off the Empire State Building, and as he passed the 42nd floor, the window washers heard him say, 'So Far, so good.'"
- *John McGahern, Leitrim author who wrote "The Barracks" and five other novels*

"He was a one-off, a unique figure of medieval power, intrigue and complexity,

surrounded by mystery and money, and protected by populism and cleverness and the well-timed one-liner."
- Maire Goeghegan-Quinn, former Irish cabinet member, speaking of three-time Irish Prime Minister Charles Haughey, who died June 13, 2006

"You know, I have a theory about Charlie Haughey. If you give him enough rope, he'll hang you."
- BBC Ireland reporter Leo Enright

"He is the best, the most skillful, the most devious and the most cunning."
- Charles Haughey's description of his successor as Prime Minister, Bertie Ahern

"A fox on your fishing hook."
- Irish curse

"Could he not find in his heart the generosity to acknowledge that there is a small nation that stood alone not for one year or two, but for several hundred years against aggression; that endured spoliations, famines, massacres in endless succession; that was clubbed many times into insensibility, but that each time on returning

89

[to] consciousness took up the fight anew; a small nation that could never be got to accept defeat and has never surrendered her soul?"
- *Eamon De Valera, on Victory Day in Europe, May 8, 1945, responding to criticism by Winston Churchill of Ireland's neutrality in World War II, a speech in which De Valera also thanked Churchill for not invading Ireland*

"Though I soon became typecast in Hollywood as a gangster and hoodlum, I was originally a dancer, an Irish hoofer, trained in vaudeville tap dance. I always leapt at the opportunity to dance in films later on."
- *James Cagney*

"If you could drink dreams like the Irish streams
Then the world would be high as the mountain of morn
In the Pool they told us the story
How the English divided the land..."
- *John Lennon, "The Luck of the Irish" (song)*

"In some of these institutions the buildings were designedly rendered gloomy by the windows being obscured, so that the

inmates were severed from the outside
world almost as effectively as if they were in
prison."
*- From a report on Ireland's Magdalene Asylums
published in 1907 by a humanitarian group from
London*

"A doctor's reputation is made by the
number of eminent men who die under his
care."
- George Bernard Shaw

"Well, it takes all kinds of men to build a
railroad."
"No sir, just us Irish."
*- Railroad barons in "Dodge City," Warner Bros.,
1939*

"I saw a fleet of fishing boats...I flew down
almost touching the craft and yelled at them,
asking if I was on the right road to Ireland.
They just stared. Maybe they didn't hear me.
Maybe I didn't hear them. Or maybe they
thought I was just a crazy fool."
- Charles Lindbergh

"The most important thing to remember
about drunks is that drunks are far more

intelligent than non-drunks. They spend a lot of time talking in pubs, unlike workaholics who concentrate on their careers and ambitions, who never develop their higher spiritual values, who never explore the insides of their head like a drunk does."

- Shane MacGowen, lead singer/ songwriter for The Pogues

"I only drink on two occasions – When I am thirsty and when I'm not thirsty."
- Brendan Behan

"Neither Christ nor Buddha nor Socrates wrote a book, for to do so is to exchange life for a logical process."
- William Butler Yeats

"Beware of the man whose God is in the skies."
- George Bernard Shaw

"I am a drinker with a writing problem."
- Brendan Behan

"You know its summer in Ireland when the rain gets warmer."
- *Hal Roach*

"Aim at heaven and you will get earth thrown in. Aim at earth and you get neither."
- *C. S. Lewis*

"As I walked back to the car, I chatted with an Englishman, who confirmed that, indeed, sheep are dropping into the oceans around Ireland at a regular rate."
- *Margeret Lynn McLean, noting the general lack of fences along cliff edges on Irish farms, "Insights on Ireland"*

"He comes from a brainy Cork Family."
- *First line of a British police dossier on Michael Collins, discovered by Collins himself during a raid on Dublin Castle*

"Unlike almost every other Irish revolutionary, he was successful."
- *Irish-American author Dermot McEvoy, on why Michael Collins is such a revered figure in Ireland*

"There is, for whatever reason, an international tendency to be well-disposed towards Ireland - a tendency that elevates us beyond our actual standing on the world stage."
- *Ivana Bacik, Irish barrister and Labour Party politician*

"Though the pen is mightier than the sword, the sword speaks louder and stronger at any given moment."
- *Leonard Wibberley, Irish author of comic novel "The Mouse That Roared"*

"This is one race of people for whom psychoanalysis is of no use whatsoever."
- *Sigmund Freud (speaking about the Irish)*

"Ireland, sir, for good or evil, is like no other place under heaven, and no man can touch its sod or breathe its air without becoming better or worse."
- *George Bernard Shaw*

"Every absurdity has a champion to defend it."
- *Oliver Goldsmith*

"For the good are always the merry,
Save for an evil chance,
And the merry love the fiddle,
And the merry love to dance"
- W.B. Yeats, "The Fiddler of Dooney"

"I used to go missing quite allot...Miss Canada, Miss United Kingdom, Miss World."
- Soccer Superstar George Best

"Anyone under 35 feels like they are going through a meat grinder...It's almost as if the economy is eating its young."
- Eddie Hobbs, host of the popular Irish TV show "Rip-Off Republic"

"I started with rock n' roll and...then you start to take it apart like a child with a toy and you see there's blues and there's country...Then you go back from country into American music...and you end up in Scotland and Ireland eventually."
- Elvis Costello

"Those who drink to forget, please pay in advance."
- Sign at the Hibernian Bar, Cork City

"This day is a happy one for America. In some places Americans get a little too happy."
- *President George Bush, greeting Bertie Ahern at the White House on St. Patrick's Day 2004*

"In Manhasset you were either Yankees or Mets, rich or poor, sober or drunk...You were 'Gaelic' or 'garlic,' as one schoolmate told me, and I couldn't admit, to him or myself, that I had both Irish and Italian ancestors."
- *J. R. Moehringer, "The Tender Bar"*

"Today I come back to you as a descendant of people who were buried here in pauper's graves."
- *President Ronald Reagan, on a visit to Ballyporeen in 1984*

"The Irish gave the bagpipes to the Scotts as a joke, but the Scotts haven't seen the joke yet."
- *Oliver Herford*

"Traveling - I was all my life at it. I'd still rather be traveling around. I'm always thinking of it. It was a better and a nicer

time on the road – more freedom along the roads. We'd be selling tinware, saucepans, cans – country people knew us well at those times and were very nice."
- Former Irish Traveller (or "Tinker") Nan McDonagh

"Even if the ball was wrapped in bacon, Lassie couldn't find it."
- Heard from an Irish caddie, after a particularly bad shot

"He was the chaplain's clerk, a slender Irishman with prematurely gray hair, melancholy eyes. His voice was the glory of the prison's choir."
- Truman Capote, "In Cold Blood"

"It's easy to love humanity when you're this far away from it."
- Actor Daniel Day Lewis (who has lived in Ireland at various times), quoted while looking down from the mountains of Luggala, County Wicklow in the New York Times

"I was raised in an Irish-American home in Detroit where assimilation was the uppermost priority. The price of assimilation

and respectability was amnesia. Although my great-grandparents were victims of the Great Hunger of the 1840's, even though I was named Thomas Emmet Hayden IV after the radical Irish nationalist exile Thomas Emmet, my inheritance was to be disinherited. My parents knew nothing of this past, or nothing worth passing on."
- *Tom Hayden*

"The worst threat to Irish farmers is not foot and mouth disease, but a postal strike."
- *Popular saying in rural Ireland, referring to Irish farmers' heavy dependence on government subsidy checks to survive*

"As a writer, I write to see. If I knew how it would end, I wouldn't write. It's a process of discovery."
- *Author John McGahern*

"The great Gaels of Ireland are the men that God made mad. For all their wars are merry, and all their songs are sad."
- *G.K. Chesterton*

"Ireland, thou friend of my country in my country's most friendless days, much

injured, much enduring land, accept this poor tribute from one who esteems thy worth, and mourns thy desolation."
- *George Washington, speaking of Ireland's support for America during the revolution*

"I tell you this – early this morning I signed my death warrant."
- *Michael Collins, after signing a treaty on December 6, 1921 with England creating the Irish Free State as a dominion within the British Commonwealth. He was later assassinated by partisans unhappy with the deal.*

"If (my grandfather) hadn't left, I'd be working over here at the Albatross Company."
- *JFK, during a 1963 visit to Ireland*

"A wise man should have money in his head, but not in his heart."
- *Jonathan Swift*

"When anyone asks me about the Irish character, I say look at the trees – maimed, stark and misshapen, but ferociously tenacious."
- *Edna O'Brien*

"A man who is not afraid of the sea will soon be drowned...for he will go out on a day he shouldn't. But we do be afraid of the sea, and we only be drownded now and again."
- John Millington Synge, in his book "The Aran Islands," 1907

"Failures are finger posts on the road to achievement."
- C. S. Lewis

"I'll tell you what you can expect from an Irishman named Wellington whose father was a bookmaker. You can expect that anything he says or writes may be repeated aloud in your own home in front of your children. You can believe he was taught to love and respect all mankind, but to fear no man."
- The late Wellington Mara, owner of the New York Giants, responding to a sportswriter's criticism

"I have never seen a West Cork farmer with an umbrella, except at a funeral. His father or grandfather, who went to the creamery with an ass and cart, insulated himself against the vagaries of the heavens with a

thick woolen overcoat and slightly greasy flat cap. Little rain permeated the oxter or the headgear. Beneath the outer layer, which could weigh a hundredweight when well soaked, the man remained dry and warm."
- *Damien Engright, "A Place Near Heaven – A Year in West Cork"*

"It is a curious contradiction, not very often remembered in England, that for many generations the private soldiers of the British Army were largely Irish."
- *Cecil Woodham-Smith*

"There is no language like the Irish for soothing and quieting."
- *John Millington Synge*

"As an intending Trappist, he would have to turn his back on pleasure but that would not be so easy because he knew of practically nothing which could be called pleasure."
- *Flan O'Brien, "The Dalkey Archive"*

"It's not that the Irish are cynical. It's simply that they have a wonderful lack of respect for everything and everybody."
- *Brendan Behan*

"The isles of Aran are fameous for the numerous multitude of Saints there living of old and interred..."
- *Roderick O'Flaherty, 1684*

"Take care to get what you like or you will be forced to like what you get."
- *George Bernard Shaw*

"When I told the people of Northern Ireland that I was an atheist, a woman in the audience stood up and said, 'Yes, but is it the God of the Catholics or the God of the Protestants in whom you don't believe?'"
- *Quentin Crisp*

"There can be no tradition without innovation."
- *Earle Hitchner, Irish music journalist*

"There is always a right and a wrong way, and the wrong way always seems more reasonable."
- *George Moore, Irish novelist*

"If there is music in hell it will be bagpipes."
- *Joe Tomelty, Irish actor and playwright*

Cobh, Near Cork City

"What was it that made Maggie leave
Ireland, forsake her siblings and parents and
flee to New York in the 1800s, we never
knew. We yearned to know, because she was
the first in a long line of leavers, the
matriarch of a clan of men and women who
made mysterious and dramatic exits. But her
reason for leaving must have been too
awful, too painful, because Maggie was said
to be a born storyteller, and that story was
the one she would never tell."
- *J.R. Moehringer, "The Tender Bar"*

8 Offbeat Irish News Stories

The Old Sod On Mars?

An Irish science professor who played around with bog plants has found that her odd interest has put her on NASA's research team. Michelle Bennett, who heads the Limerick Institute of Technology's Applied Science Department, stuck some samples of Irish bog fauna into airtight jars, put them in a garage and then forgot about them. A year later, she came across them again, opened them up and was surprised to discover they were all still alive. She approached the American space agency with the idea of testing the hearty sphagnum mosses to create self-sustaining sources of food and water on spaceships, and more specifically for future use on a mission to Mars. NASA now has her working on the project for them.

Naked People And Wild Escapades About To Appear On Irish Screens!

The Irish Film Censor's Office, which over the years cut or outlawed movies including Gone With The Wind, Casablanca and Midnight Cowboy, found itself cut recently when it was folded into another government agency. In its heyday, it was a force to be reckoned with. In 1923, its first head censor, one Mr. James Montgomery, banned 124 films. According to *The Irish Times*, Montgomery happily proclaimed that he knew absolutely nothing about movies. He simply consulted the Ten Commandments (not the Charlton Heston version) for guidance on them.

Talk About Clean

Eyeries, a colorful little village on the Beara Peninsula in County Cork, was named Ireland's "Best Kept Town" in 2012. If you love squeaky clean places you might want to visit Eyeries and previous winners Lismore (County Waterford), Killarney (County Kerry), Emly (County Tipperary) or Westport (County Mayo).

Forever Hurling

71-year-old Tom Randles of Tullylease, County Cork, is clearly still ready to take a whack at the ball, and at anyone who gets in his way. The lifelong hurler, who once won an All-Ireland medal in the rough and tumble sport, recently filled in for a missing player on a team in the Junior A League. The grandfather, who frequently works out with the hurling team, also stays fit by walking and dancing. Mr. Randles played the full 60 minutes of the match at the corner forward position.

Guinness Brews Less At St. James Gate

All true lovers of stout know that St. James Gate in Dublin is the global center of the Guinness brewing empire. And while Diagio, the conglomerate that now owns Guinness, isn't planning to skip out on the 9,000-year lease the company signed on the property in 1759, it looks as though the St. James Gate brewery is going to become more of a tourist site and less of a true brewery. Much of the brewing activities at the old site will be moved to other plants Guinness operates around Ireland, including a modern, efficient one being built near

Dublin. Though the famous Guinness tour, which attracts some 900,000 visitors per year, will continue, numerous workers at the old plant could be in line to lose their jobs. A portion of the St. James Gate property is to be redeveloped, but another chunk will be sold off.

Island of Empty Cars

Arranmore Island, off the coast of Donegal, has a problem that may become common in America when gas reaches $10 a gallon. It seems as though tourists who visit the remote, beautiful outpost are in the habit of simply abandoning their cars when they run out of petrol. Over the years, more than 500 rusting hulks of automobiles have built up the island, which is only a few miles across. The local government has now dragged all the derelict vehicles back to Sligo on the mainland, where they are being crushed for recycling.

High On Love – Really, Really High

A helicopter pilot from Cashel literally bet the farm on his marriage proposal recently, plowing a huge message into a farm field asking his lady love to be accept his troth.

His girlfriend, awakened at 7:30 am and taken on a surprise helicopter ride, apparently reacted well when she looked out the window and saw the proposal cut into wheat far below. The pilot, keeping one hand firmly on the controls, managed to pull out a ring to complete the proposal, which was accepted.

Gang Truce in Stab City

Two gangs who rank as the Hatfields and McCoys of Limerick, known as the Keane/Collopy and McCarthy/Dundon gangs, have reportedly made an agreement to stop fighting on the heels of a wave of violence that took ten lives. With the help of two "non-criminal intermediaries," according to Irish Emmigrant, the two groups have put their feud aside, at least for the moment.

Judges With Bad Blarney

Irish judges seem to be excelling these days at the art of sticking their feet in their mouths. In one recent incident, a judge suspended most of the five-year sentence of a County Waterford man convicted of raping a 26-year-old prostitute from Croatia.

The judge made headlines for saying he felt the suspended sentence was appropriate because the Waterford man, a father of six who visits prostitutes frequently, is "a man of good character." Not long afterward, a Monaghan judge managed to offend an entire Irish county. When a student from County Tyrone said she had only obsolete sterling on hand to pay the standard €50 fine to have her case thrown out of court (a common but questionable practice in Irish courts), Judge Sean McBride said she was showing "the typical thickness of Tyrone people." The judge later apologized, claiming that his lack of tact was the result of a "long tiring day."

The Harlot's Name Remains The Same
Long running efforts by residents of Doon, County Limerick, to bring back a name that was taken from their town in 2003 appear to have succeeded. The town has been known as "Dun Bleisce" as far back as 774. Problem is, that's believed to translate into "Fort of the Harlot." In 2003, The Irish Placenames Commission decided that decent little towns shouldn't be named after harlots, and changed the name to "An

Dun," which apparently doesn't mean much of anything. That set off a grand etymological debate, with some claiming that Dun Bleisce means "the stronghold of immoral women," and others saying that "harlot" once meant "powerful women." (How else could they have a fort?). After some 800 locals signed a petition to bring back the old name, the Placenames Commission director has issued an order to bring back the name Dun Bleisce.

Ryanair Plays Hardball With Rugby Fans

Faced with a tough economic climate, cut-rate Irish airline Ryanair apparently decided to push the concept of fluid pricing to the max. Irish rugby fans who bought tickets far ahead of time to Bristol, England for finals of the European cup were thrilled when their team qualified for the big game – and then aggravated when they found that their Ryanair flight had suddenly been cancelled (they were offered refunds or alternative flights). Oddly enough, the same flight shortly re-appeared on the airline's schedule, but with ticket prices six times as high as the rugby fans had originally paid. Michael

O'Leary, Ryanair's CEO, said that the airline had not been closely watching the rugby standings, and the whole thing was a technical mix up. The fans ultimately got free air tickets to travel to the big game.

Mangled Oscar Acceptance
Apparently those 12 years of Gaelic language that every Irish kid is required to take in school isn't enough to teach 'em to speak good. Dublin-bred Glen Hansard, who's "Falling Slowly" from indie film "Once" earned him an Oscar for best song in 2008, apparently made a bit of a Gaelic boo-boo in front of a huge TV audience. *The New York Times* reports that in trying to say "Thanks a million" to the academy, he said "go raibh, mile, maith agat." Unfortunately "agat" is singular, and should have been "agaibh." No word yet on whether Mr. Hansard's primary school diploma will be revoked.

No Cells Allowed In Cellblocks
Denis Kelly of County Cork has the odd distinction of being the first prisoner in Ireland ever convicted of having a cell phone in jail. Possessing a mobile phone in

Irish prison today can result in a fine of up to 5,000 Euros, and a sentence of five (additional) years in jail.

Blarney Stone Bru Ha-Ha

A new book by two archaeologists from Britain has caused a minor furor over whether or not that piece of rock that tourists line up to plant their lips on in Blarney Castle is actually the real Blarney stone. Authors Mark Samuel and Kate Hamlyn say the true Blarney stone is actually somewhere else in the famous County Cork castle. Sir Charles Colthurst, the current owner of the castle, says they're wrong. Though the approach to the stone was changed some years ago for safety purposes, he argues, the much-smootched rock is the real item. In case you're wondering, there are two versions of the legend of how the Blarney Stone came into being. The first is that Cormac MacCarthy, owner of the castle during the reign of Queen Elizabeth I, was extraordinarily skilled at never giving the queen what she wanted. Every request she made of MacCarthy was met with long-winded elaborations and bluffs, to the point where the "Virgin Queen" yelled out one day, "This is all Blarney, he never says what he means!" Version number two is that a magic stone was built into the castle in the 1400's, but no one knew exactly where. When one of the castle's owners found a witch drowning in a river and saved her, she told him where the magic stone was, and that kissing it would give anyone the power of persuasion evermore.

Irish Immigrants Return To U.S.
In additional economic news, The Irish Times reports that there has been a new influx of Irish immigrants coming into the United States since the start of 2008. The reason: Ireland's economy has weakened, making jobs there more difficult to find.

No More Rings In Barmbrack Cakes?
You would think that a recent EU ban on toys or other foreign objects being included in food product packaging would upset only the makers of Cracker Jacks. But the Irish don't like it because one of the oldest traditions in the Celtic world is to bake a ring into the Halloween "barmbrack" cake, and declare that whoever bites into it will soon get married, come into money or enjoy

good luck of some other type. Apparently, only homemade barmbracks will carry on this tradition henceforth.

Irish Get Used To Welcoming Immigrants

Ireland's economic success in the 1990's attracted lots of immigrants, particularly from Eastern Europe. At times, that's been a bit of a problem for Irish folk, most of whom grew up in the very homogenous environment that existed in the country until the early 1980's. Reports have popped up in newspapers of immigrants feeling they were being discriminated against or treated rudely in Ireland. But apparently, most Irish people feel the new arrivals are a plus for the island. According to a survey conducted by the European Union in 2008, over 80% of people in Ireland feel that the nation's cultural life has been improved by the arrival of new immigrants.

No "Get Out Of Jail" Card Needed

You may have stayed in castles, but you haven't lived until you've spent a night in prison. Under a proposal by a Dublin area developer, you could soon have the chance to do so, while being taken care of by a concierge instead of a prison guard. The Dublin City Council is considering a plan to convert 19th century Mountjoy Prison into a boutique hotel, as part of a larger plan to repurpose the government-owned property that includes the prison and several other old buildings. The building has wrought iron gates and numerous other old-world features, though the windows are said to be a bit on the small side. One small obstacle: the prison is currently full of, well, prisoners. Remodeling can begin after they are moved to a new facility in 2011.

St. Everywhere But Ireland

If you go to a hospital in Ireland these days, don't expect to hear your nurses speaking in that familiar Irish brogue – or in any other European language for that matter. The Royal College of Surgeons in Ireland reports that over 50% of all new nurses registered in The Republic in 2006 were not only from outside Ireland, but outside the European Union.

Don't Drink The Irish Water?

Ireland's historically weak enforcement of

environmental standards caused major problems with drinking water during the Celtic Tiger era, as a building boom spread new houses willy-nilly across the landscape. At the same time, some technology industry folks referred to Ireland simply as "the ghetto," because unregulated production of CDs and other computer products were creating so much toxic waste in the country. In 2007, the issue was brought into focus by a water-borne disease outbreak in Galway that sickened over 240 people, and caused a "boil water rule" to be imposed for five months. That same year, the EU Environment Commissions Stavros Dimas warned that many town water supplies showed a presence of E. coli. Smart travelers are still advised to avoid ice cubes and stick to bottled water in Irish rural areas, and generally avoid water from kitchen and bathroom sinks.

Guinness Heist

A "low tech" thief with lots of moxie stole more than 450 kegs (about 40,000 bottles worth) of Guinness from the main factory in Dublin recently. The fellow, who has not been found as yet, simply backed a truck into the yard at the St. James Gate Facility, hitched up a trailer full of the brown stuff, and drove off unmolested. The trailer, minus the Guinness, was later discovered in the countryside.

Make Mine Cavan - Not The Other Cola
You've seen defunct beer brands come back in recent years, but what about old soft drinks? Apparently, hearts, or at least one heart, in County Cavan yearned for an old drink called "Cavan Cola" that was made from 1984 until the 1990's, when its manufacturer was sold. In 2007, Mr. Don Leahy sought to rekindle interest in the sweet concoction by creating a website and a T-shirt for it. It drew considerable attention to Mr. Leahy, who told *The Irish Times* that he wanted to bring the drink back because "Cavan Cola is a forgotten symbol of what Cavan stood for - Cavan Cola defines refreshment, coolness and vintage Cavan culture." Apparently, one key element in the drink's popularity was the fact that when poured in a glass, it had a frothy head that allowed young bucks to pretend they were imbibing Guinness. At the time of this book's new printing in 2013, all mentions of

Cavan Cola seemed to have disappeared from the media.

A Company That Finds Water The Old-Fashioned Way

Brand new company Clare Spring Water Ltd. will draw its product from three top quality springs that were found the old fashioned way. Local government official P.J. Kelly seems to have proved that he has a talent for "divining." Not long ago he took a coat hanger and went out into the countryside looking for water, something he says he has been able to do for over forty years. Sure enough, Kelly located three water sources big enough to support a new company that's going to employ 10 people. He says he discovered his talent for finding water when he picked up a pair of tongs and felt a shock go through them.

Statue, But No Cake, Left Out In The Rain In Limerick

Dublin has its statue of Molly Malone, and now Limerick has a bronze reproduction of favorite son Richard Harris. The life size piece by Jim Connolly, an artist who also happens to be known in Ireland as an advocate of housing development in the countryside (much like the people Mr. Harris did battle with in "The Field") was unveiled in front of Harris first wife and three sons. Harris was known for his starring roles in "Camelot" and for his mega pop hit "McArthur Park."

Saving Kerry's Stone Walls

A controversy has arisen about plans to put up precast concrete barriers along many parts of the Ring of Kerry. Irish Minister for the Environment John Gormley is complaining that the modern barriers will destroy the scenic vistas along the crowded tourist route.

Goat Rescue

A group of goats who make their home on Bilberry Rock in Waterford are very lucky quadrupeds. Two sisters who have lived near the rock since childhood, Ann and Orla Foley, have long taken it upon themselves to feed and look after the goats. But goat food and veterinary costs are going up these days like everything else. Around the time of our first printing in 2007, the Foley sisters set up the "Bilberry Goat Heritage Trust" to collect the 100 or so Euros needed each year to feed the animals during the winter. Happily, the trust and the goats are still going strong. You can donate to it at: http://www.bilberrygoatheritagetrust.com.

St. Paddy's Day Will Cost Ya
Keep an eye on your hotel bill if you visit Dublin around Saint Patrick's Day. *The Journal.ie* reports that in 2013, the average rate for Saturday March 16th (the night before Dublin's parade), the average hotel room is going for $400., versus a typical average rate of $140. for the rest of March.

Last Irish Warrior Standing
The very last known veteran of the Irish War of Independence, Republican Dan Keating, died in October of 2007. The War of Independence, or Anglo-Irish War, arose in the wake of the 1916 uprising, and raged from 1919 until 1921.

Even Non-Human Athletes Are "Juicing"
Though it's truly more sad than funny, a recent report by an Irish government committee charged that greyhound owners

are feeding cocaine to their dogs to enhance performance. No word yet on whether the dogs are being offered major league baseball contracts.

The Sea Still Claims Fishermen
Even in modern Ireland, the fishermen who ply the sea still face old dangers. One recent accident claimed the lives of a father and son team of fishermen from Inver, County Donegal. The two were out for lobsters in Donegal Bay when the weather deteriorated. Other fisherman became worried about the Kennedy's when they did not return to port. Though a Coast Guard helicopter quickly found the two clinging to each other in the water, they died not long after from hypothermia in the local hospital. They had spent about two hours in the cold Atlantic waters.

No Hurry To Get To The Altar
Irish people are waiting longer to get married, and getting might choosy about who they'll tie the knot with, according the Central Statistics Office. The average bride in Ireland is now 31 years old, while the typical groom is 33 (men in farming

communities tend to wait longer, marrying at an average age of 35). Irish people, according to the study, are now less inclined than they once were to make a commitment unless they have found an "idealized person."

Free Chops
Some Irish sheep farmers have found a friendly, positive way to protest the low price they are getting for their product. A group of them got a rousing welcome as they passed out free lamb chops in the center of Dublin.

Glad To Give Hours of Legal Advice
The eyes of Irish lawyers must be shining. Besides the fact that people in Ireland are suing each other like crazy, hourly rates are getting better all the time. Under a new ruling by the Irish Master of the High Court, barristers will all get a minimum hourly rate of 100 Euros.

Bertie Never Had A Bong
It was a Clintonesque moment when Ireland's Prime Minister (now former prime minister) found it necessary to deny that he

ever went through a "Bertie the hippie" phase. Mr. Ahern was squirming a bit, perhaps, after his Minister for Finance, Brian Cowen, freely admitted in an interview that he had smoked pot several times as a university student in the 1970's. Ahern firmly denied that he had ever inhaled even the smallest bit of marijuana at any time in his life.

Exactly What Award Was That?

Conservative cable show host Bill O'Reilly bloviated a bit, perhaps, when he visited Ireland a few years ago. One night during the trip, he phoned into his own show, which was being hosted by a substitute, to say he was "getting a big award" from the Irish Philosophical Society. He was, in fact, only delivering a speech to the group.

Down On The Hollywood Farm

The local gentry in Kilteevan, County Roscommon, were buzzing a few years back about Tom Cruise's apparent desire to purchase his family's ancestral farm there. The actor visited the area whilst tracing his Irish ancestry, and his agents were allegedly negotiating to buy the 33-acre property once owned by the Mapother family. Cruise's proper name is "Tom Cruise Mapother IV." Cruise ultimately lost interest in the property, which is probably a good thing. Genealogists have now determined that the actor's ancestor merely adopted the Mapother name, which means that he was not actually related to the family that owned the farm.

Nice Pipes
The Dublin City Council is in the habit of using scantily clad models at promotional events, and Ireland's Green Party isn't happy about it. Green Party Women's Affairs spokesperson Cllr Brownen Maher has complained about the Council's use of "glamour" girls. As an example, she noted one event where two models in mini-skirts were hired to appear at a press conference promoting plans to replace decaying water pipes in Dublin. Ms. Maher says the use of attractive young women to draw attention to government events is "clichéd and old-fashioned."

Blasted Fairies Again
Outside Killarney, there's a dip that keeps

appearing in the N22 no matter how many times road crews try to fix it. One local politician, a Mr. Danny Healy-Rae, thinks he knows what's causing the problem: fairies. The area, after all, is surrounded by Celtic stones and monuments, and some local township names refer to "lioses," or fairy forts. Local highway department officials have yet to buy into the fairy concept. They claim the dip keeps reappearing because of a "geotechnical" problem.

Tree of Strife
Yet another battle has been fought in the ongoing war between Irish road builders and fairies (or the supporters of fairies, at least). On the heels of a headline-making tale about a dip that keeps appearing in a road outside Killarney because of angry spirits, a "magic tree" in Latoon, County Clare, became a cause célèbre among spiritualists. Plans to make way for a bypass by cutting down the tree, which was allegedly an ancient meeting place for fairies on their way back from battles in western Ireland, have been widely protested by locals. The government says it will now back down and build the road around the tree.

Neither Rain Nor Sleet Nor Iceberg

A set of keys from the Titanic's mailroom, recovered from the body of one of the workers who died there, recently fetched 147,000 Euro at an auction in London. *The Irish Times* saw this as a fitting moment to memorialize an Irish postal worker, James Bertram Williamson, who lost his life in the disaster. The ship's postal workers - all five of whom perished - were seen trying to haul heavy sacks of mail up from the hold, refusing to put down their work to save themselves. Titanic enthusiasts will recall that the mail room, close to the ship's bow, was one of the first places to go under. Crewmembers above it on the ship's foredeck recall the air vents whistling because incoming water was forcing oxygen up out of the ship so quickly. In the black and white movie "A Night To Remember," architect Thomas Andrews goes below to inspect the iceberg damage, and is told by an excited crewmember that "the mail hold's flooded already." *The Irish Times* reports that families of three of the mail workers who were Americans will each get $2,000 from the proceeds of the auction. It's unclear if Mr. Williamson's family will get anything.

Swimming Footballs & Ducks

Ever hear that story about the message in a bottle? Well, *The Irish Times* made room to report on a football (which some might call a soccer ball) kicked into the River Dargle in Bray by the coach of a county team. The ball was eventually found by a gentleman on the Isle of Man, near England. Because the ball had the coach's phone number written on it, the man was able to return it. He noted that other items from Ireland frequently wash up on the shores of the Isle of Man, particularly large numbers of plastic ducks from the annual duck race in the River Liffey.

Four Very, Very Productive Irish Employees

Ever wonder how Ireland got so rich during the Celtic Tiger era? Well, one reason is the fact that corporate taxes there were, and still are, incredibly low. Unfortunately, this has encouraged some American companies to do more than make widgets there. California tech company SanDisk was called out a few years back for funneling almost a billion dollars in revenue through a subsidiary in Ireland that had just four employees. Amazingly, the company appears to be in little trouble for this bit of creative bookkeeping. "It's no different from any other holding company," Hugh Connolly of SanDisk told *The Irish Times.* "Most international companies have that kind of holding company structure."

The View From This Cliff Is Just...ahhhhhhhh!

The Irish government has cut a deal with farmers, so they can feel comfortable about hikers strolling across their land. Under the new "Countryside Walkways Scheme," farmers will be paid about 1,000 Euro per year each to let the public onto paths that have criss-crossed their land for decades. The deal includes an indemnification against lawsuits – a key provision for farmers who fear lawsuits from people who hurt themselves on their land. One case in 2003 resulted in a Donegal farmer being ordered to pony up 84,000 Euro to a woman who fell off a cliff. The Irish Supreme court later overturned that award, making a common sense observation (almost unthinkable today in the U.S. court system) that the woman should have known it was dangerous to walk up to the edge of a cliff.

Dublin Looking More Like Los Angeles

The number of cars in Dublin today is double what it was just 15 years ago, *The New York Times* reports. Since 1990, emissions from cars and other transportation means have risen 140 per cent.

Ireland Rules At Least A Few Waves

The Irish government announced its biggest-ever military equipment contract, stating that three new vessels will be built for its navy at a cost of 180 million Euros. This will bring the total size of Ireland's navy to 11 boats. According to the Irish Navy's website, the fleet also includes a few "inflatable craft."

Government Pub Crawl

Commuters to Dublin may have to struggle through three hours of traffic each way, but people in the countryside can now count on a quick ride to the pub, courtesy of the Irish government. A free service to ferry people back and forth to pubs will now be offered to those who live in isolated areas not served by busses or taxis.

West Coast View

Nobody Home

Up until the economic crash of 2008, Irish
home builders were refusing to rent empty
homes because prices were rising so fast and
offers were coming in so hot and heavy that
they didn't want to lock themselves into
even short term rental leases. Now they
would be glad to rent out any of the 200,000
vacant new homes in the country. But with
over $225 billion in real estate liabilities on
Ireland's books today - about $51,000 for
every man, woman and child in the nation -
the list of renters and purchasers has
shrunken to virtually zero.

Mystery of the Deep

A team of amateur Irish divers who recently dove the wreck of the Lusitania in the Irish Sea claim to have found munitions in its cargo hold. The sinking of the Lusitania by a German submarine is considered the key event that brought America into World War One. Historians have argued ever since about whether the ship sank so quickly – in less than 25 minutes – because of the torpedo itself or because of explosions it triggered of American ammunition being secretly transported inside the ship to European allies.

Out Of Songs - And Teeth As Well

Shane MacGowan, former singer for the mildly famous group The Pogues, has built a unique kind of fame in Ireland over the past decade or two. No longer in the musical game, MacGowan now makes the Irish papers regularly for his drinking exploits, but even more, for his dental problems. A man who once possessed the most multi-directional smile this side of David Bowie (who finally got them straightened a few years back), MacGowan's celebrity is now based on how regularly he loses a tooth during a pub crawl. *The Irish Post*, apparently hard up for real news, has reported that he fell off a wall outside a pub in Kilcurry (County Limerick), resulting in the loss of two more pearly whites. The dental yarn may be almost run, however, as a friend of MacGowan's reports that at this point, "he hasn't got that many left teeth to lose."

Waiting For A Train
The increasing popularity of commuting to work by train has created a huge snarl on Ireland's limited railroad system. To deal with the mess, Iarnród Éireann's has come up with an incredibly complicated new series of schedules. An unfortunate result is that several trips now actually take longer than they did 20 years ago.

Yeats Family Mixed Literature And Politics
Former Irish senator Michael Yeats died recently at the age of 86. Yeats, who served as the first Irish vice-president of the European Parliament, was the son of famed poet W.B. Yeats. In between writing couplets, the father also served as an Irish senator (W.B. Yeats died in 1939).

Irish - the New Language of Bureaucracy

The European Union recently accepted Irish as one of its official languages. This follows a long campaign to get the old language accepted by Bertie Ahern. Irish newspaper writers were quick to point out that having the EUs new regulations translated into Irish means that even fewer Irish people will probably read them, since most consider the national requirement to learn Irish in grammar school a waste of time.

Too Much Dublin Luxury

Managers of SAS Hotels, which runs the five-star St. Helens Hotel on Stillorgan Road, are saying that there are now too many luxury hotels in Dublin. Government tax breaks set off a hotel building spree a few years ago that has, according to the most recent SAS financial filing, created a situation where "the five-star hotel market in Dublin and the sensitive tourism market present a very challenging period for the hotel's sales." Don't expect any big breaks on your five-star room rate, however. In spite of allegedly having too much competition, SAS and the St. Helens are still managing to charge well over 200 Euros per night for a room.

The White Woman's Burden
Just in case you thought it was only Irish men who liked to drink too much, a study by a University College of London Professor shows that Irish women engage in "binge drinking" four times or more every fortnight (two weeks). That makes them heavier drinkers than either Irish men or other females in Europe.

Pub Culture The Only Culture
Immigrants to Ireland like the fact that people are friendly and there are lots of social welfare benefits, according to a study by The National Action Plan Against Racism. The main problems that immigrants say they run into include Ireland being surprisingly expensive and dirty, and that it has too much drug use and too many street beggars. Newcomers also say they find "the dominance of pub culture as almost the only social outlet very strange."

Irish Halloween: A Little Too Exciting
Halloween holds a place of honor on the

Celtic calendar. But modern day Halloween is not without its problems on the emerald isle. On one recent Halloween night, over 380 fire calls were made in Dublin, while all sorts of egg throwing and property damage incidents occurred. *RTE* reported that in Longford, a small number of "youths from dysfunctional families" barricaded themselves inside a small local authority housing estate and terrorized residents by, among other things, "breaking windows and pulling up shrubs."

The Greatest Irish Person You Never Heard Of

A recent poll shows that people in Wicklow believe that the single greatest person in the entire history of Ireland was Anne Devlin. In case this name doesn't ring a bell with you, Anne Devlin was a housekeeper to Irish revolutionary Robert Emmett in the early 1800's. Devlin's real job was not to keep the house clean, but to provide an appearance of normality to a building that was constantly being visited by Emmett's conspirators. Arrested by British authorities, Devlin was tortured and kept with her entire family in a prison so squalid that her young brother died there. Even though Emmett urged her to confess to her anti-British activities to save herself, she refused to inform on any of the Irish revolutionaries. Released from prison in 1806, she died in poverty in 1851.

The West No Longer The Best
In spite of Ireland's general economic success these days, the government is allowing rural Western Ireland to suffer serious declines. At least that's the claim made in a report by the Western Development Commission, a government body that's supposed to promote social and economic development in The West. According to the group's report, there is an ongoing decline in both population and prosperity in rural areas because the government has cut back on money for development of the region. It's hard to know how accurate the Commission's claims are, since private and public groups have used similar language to promote unlimited home-building in rural Ireland in the past.

100+ Basking Sharks Off County Kerry

The Irish Examiner reports that several people report seeing large numbers of sharks near Valentia Island, off the Ring of Kerry. The creatures are actually not unusual in Irish waters. Basking sharks, which like to feed on plankton, have also been sighted off Donegal, while whales are often seen off Ireland's east and west coasts.

A Horse Of A Different Species

It's great that a story like this can still make headlines in Ireland. *The Limerick Post* reported recently that a local horse trainer has been turning the heads of motorists throughout the city by strolling around with his new zebra. Johnny Cross says he bought the one-year old animal in Holland recently as a curiosity, and to see if he could successfully break it (a supposed impossibility with this species). Efforts to tame the zebra have gone, well, not too badly. Says Cross, "He's as good as you could expect for a zebra." The horse trainer says he has no intention of trying to race his new pet.

With gas and oil prices going through the roof, good old turf is looking like a more attractive fuel in Ireland.
There's a significant increase in the number of people digging up bog turf for burning in West Donegal, in particular, *The Irish Emigrant* reports. Restrictions on where turf can be cut and even on the tools used for it, however, could limit the extent to which that beautiful smell will make a comeback in Irish villages.

It seems hard to believe that drinking was ever a taboo subject in Ireland.
But Lee Dunne's book "Paddy Maguire is Dead" was actually banned there in the 1970's because its account of alcoholism was considered too graphic (the author's response to the ban back then was to hand out one hundred copies for free on Grafton Street in Dublin). Only now is Mr. Dunne's book being published in Ireland, by Killynon House Books.

Multi-national companies still investing in Ireland.
Ireland's corporate tax rate of 12.5% is so low compared to other European countries

that German and French politicians have complained that it creates an unfair advantage for the Emerald Isle in terms of attracting foreign companies. The Irish know that this is exactly the idea, and in spite of cutting the minimum wage and hiking taxes on homeowners since the economic collapse of 2008, they've kept the super-low corporate tax rates in place. As a result, high tech companies including Google, Facebook and Twitter have established major offices in Dublin. In spite of the Irish government's desperate need to raise revenue, it's unlikely that this corporate perk is going to disappear any time soon. Philip R. Lane, professor of international macroeconomics at Trinity College has said in a *New York Times* interview that "In the context of a devastated economy, where it's the only thing driving the multinational sector, trying to tweak that (tax) rate is not something that any of the political parties want to do."

Get One Free What?

At the height of the economic downturn in 2008, several desperate auto dealers in Dublin and Galway teamed up with an online company to offer cars on a "buy one, get one free" basis. Amazingly, the tactic has already been used in Britain during economic downturns, and has succeeded in moving inventory for dealers. What's not clear is whether or not it's made them any money.

Million Euro Lass

Lady boxer Katie Taylor was the toast of Ireland when she won the gold medal at the 2012 London Olympics. Her return to her hometown of Bray, County Wicklow, set off a near frenzy, with over 20,000 people turning up to greet her (there are only about 30,000 in the town). Taylor, who is a born-again Christian and a teetotaler, told reporters "I can't wait to see my granny when I get home." Said one member of the welcoming crowd, "Everybody forgets about the recession when she fights."

A Winning Whiskey

The best whiskey in the whole wide world comes from an old-style distillery in County Louth, according to the judges of the International Wine and Spirit Competition. Cooley, in Riverstown, has only been in operation since 1987. But its owners are on a mission to revive traditional Irish techniques, including the "peat smoking technique" to make both grain and malt varieties (brands include Kilbeggan and Tyrconnell). They must be doing something right. In spite of all the well-known Irish brands out there, Cooley is the first whiskey producer in Ireland to ever be named world's best by this organization.

Hard Time For A Spirit

If you were a ghost, would you want to stay in prison? Apparently there's one lurking around Castlerea Prison in County Roscommon – but only since the recent blessing of a prison burial ground by Catholic clergy. Numerous sightings of the specter and lights going on and offer without explanation are turning hardened criminals into fraidy cats. The most popular theory is that the prison is being haunted by a poor fellow who took his own life there many years ago, when the building housed a mental hospital. Meanwhile, the local Bishop recently denied that his most recent visit to Castlerea included an exorcism ceremony.

Emigration, Unfortunately, Revives

During the Celtic Tiger years, a surging economy not only ground emigration from Ireland to a virtual halt, it made the country a magnet for immigrants from other countries - particularly those in Eastern Europe. But the recent economic downturn has revived Ireland's old ghost of large-scale emigration. In 2012 more than 3,000 Irish citizens left the country each month, the highest number recorded since the famine era of the mid 1800's. Most headed to other English-speaking countries such as Britain, America and Australia.

One Irish Family Multiplies In Britain

One the biggest families in England apparently came from Ireland. The vast clan was on display in the Manchester suburb of Salford recently at the funeral of its leading lady, one Ms. Margaret Ward, who came over to England from Galway in the 1960's with husband Charles. The couple were certainly productive: 15 children, 172 grandchildren (every single one of whom attended the funeral), 35 great-grandchildren and 18 great-great-grandchildren.

Celtic Tiger Fades, But Baby Boom Continues

The "Celtic Tiger" era in Ireland from 1995 to 2008 brought economic growth and lots and lots of babies. The peak year of 2008 saw over 73,000 births in The Republic – the highest number since 1898. Since then, the economic picture has changed, but the urge to reproduce apparently has not. A 2012 report by the European Union's Vital Statistics Office declared that Irish women were the most fertile in the Euro Zone, with the nation on pace to have over 75,000 births. Surprisingly for a nation that was conservative and totally Catholic not long ago, over one-third of births in Ireland now take place outside of marriage.

9 What is the Meaning of "Craic"?

The Irish keep talking about craic – but have a tough time defining it.

First things first: It's pronounced "crack."

"Let's go have some craic" is the youthful cry each Saturday evening the length and breadth of the Emerald Isle. "The craic was ninety on the Isle of Man," warbles Christy Moore in a well-known ditty (ninety = mighty).

"What is this craic and why is everybody having it or looking for it?" visitors to Ireland often ask with raised eyebrows. Craic is a Gaelic word, with no exact English translation. The closest translation you find is "fun." There's the expression "ceoil agus craic," meaning "music and fun," probably once used to describe local ceilis.

Craic doesn't appear in standard English dictionaries, but enter it as a search term on Google, and 42,500 listings come up. There's obviously a lot of craic out there.

Put simply, having craic is having a good time or a laugh. However, due to an unfortunate similarity in pronunciation with a well-known and illegal narcotic substance, not everyone gets the right idea about it. Apocryphal stories abound of unlucky Irish travelers who have had their innocent search for craic misinterpreted. In one oft-told anecdote, two Irish lads on a visit to Paris saunter down the boulevard, musing out loud on what to do and good places to find some craic. Their plans for the evening are, somewhat naturellement, misunderstood by a nearby eavesdropping gendarme. "Looking for ze crack, mais non," say the gendarmes before slapping handcuffs on the unfortunate pair and whisking them off to the nearest police station where, needless to say, they do not encounter much craic that particular evening.

The meaning of craic clearly isn't found in books. Good craic is always social. So, to pin down its meaning, I headed off one Saturday evening to the bustling area of Dublin's Temple Bar, where by all accounts the craic is mighty and even downright explosive at times. Temple Bar is an area of streets on the city center's south side, between the River Liffey and Dame Street, chock full of restaurants and pubs. The area heaves at the weekend, sometimes all too literally, when the evening's excesses catch up with many party revelers.

The vast majority of those out on my "research" evening were tourists. A man with an enormous Guinness hat looked like a good candidate to provide a definition. "What's the craic and where can you find it?" I enquired. He looked back at me blankly before saying, in Italian, that he didn't understand. Hmmm.

Two girls, dressed up for a night out on the tiles, and by all appearances somewhat tanked up, meandered by. "The craic, that's crack cocaine, innit?" they giggled. They were from Blackpool. "No, we know, it's having a laugh," they reassured me before tottering off. A gentleman from London

147

also knew the expression. Pushed for a definition, he said, "it's heading into a pub on a Saturday afternoon and it's already full and everyone is on for having a good time."

An Irish Definition
Craic was more difficult to define than expected. Perhaps it was time to rope in some authentic Irish friends who could nail down the elusive concept.

"I don't have a life at the moment," moaned one friend. "Don't ask me what the craic is. I wouldn't have a clue." Another friend, reached by phone, simply laughed and answered "You can't define it. It's just something which happens. It's organic. It depends on what is happening, where you are and who's there." She turned to ask her friends. Even over the phone, the silence was deafening. "I've got a lot of blank expressions here," she said. "Fun and frolics" was the best definition they could came up with.

With or Without Drinks
A male friend thought that craic was "having a laugh, cracking jokes, having

drinks and falling down." Is a tipple necessary for good craic? From the huge amount imbibed these days in Ireland, this would seem to be the case. Another Irishman, however, pointed out that the essence of craic is good people, a buzz and the talk – with or without a few drinks.

Even for the Irish, craic is clearly hard to pin down. Define it, and you might kill it. But if pushed, we would say the essence of craic is in the talk and banter of good company, a group of people getting together having a laugh and, most of all, taking a break from being serious about life. However, it seems your best option is to visit Ireland and find the meaning of craic yourself!

Unique definitions of Craic:
According to **http://thecraic.com/tripod.com**, "The Craic is the feng shui of a se'shium" (say that 3 times fast!). "It is the combination of the music, the drink…and trying to make headway with people of the opposite sex."

Craic Technologies of Altadena, CA, makes microspectrophotometers and spectrophotometers. Who says techies don't party?

"It's just 'fun.' Craic is a very old word – my Irish-born parents used it when I was growing up in New York." **Eileen Houlihan**, Irish teacher and writer on things Irish.

"It has to be the most popular and most widely used Irish word in this wee country's history." **Suzanne Strong**, quoted on the University of Newfoundland website.

"Craic - the particular sense of esprit produced by the confluence of drink, romance and music." **Bernard Share**, author of "Slanguage, The Dictionary of Irish Slang"

"The word 'crack' or 'craic' is rapidly approaching the status of 'begorrah.' The term most commonly refers in Ireland to an atmosphere of comfortable and pervasive conviviality, a complete absence of distrust" **Terry Eagleton**, quoted on www.beyondthecommons.com

10 Unraveling Celtic Knot Meanings

Celtic knots are an Irish symbol you'll find everywhere from designer jewelry to tattoos worn by rock n' rollers to, of course, the original Book of Kells back in old Dublin. It's not clear whether Celtic knot drawings were ever meant to symbolize anything, but lots of modern people think they contain spiritual associations. The knots are incredibly popular with followers of new age religions, magic societies and all sorts of other groups who want to draw a connection with the oldest traditions of Ireland. They also look pretty cool in T-shirts.

Whether these Irish Celtic symbols were originally meant to represent anything or were just created to be pretty pictures isn't clear. The Celts, who dominated the culture of pre-Christian Ireland, simply didn't place much importance on creating records to help future generations understand their symbols.

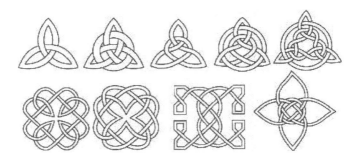

Some historians think the Celts drew them because they were prohibited from drawing any other pictures. One of the more widely accept theories to explain Celtic knot meanings says that Celtic religion, like Islam, may have prohibited realistic depictions of living creatures. This rule, which gave rise to extraordinary Arabic calligraphy, may have given birth to the complex Irish knots.

Generally, the interlaced, geometric knots fall into four categories:

Triangular or **"Triskele"** Designs

Animal Interlace: Sometimes representing men and animals intertwined, believed to represent relationships of men to women, hunters to their prey or others.

Circular Knots: Possibly symbols of cycles of life or eternity, but also seen as a sign of unity. The "endless" quality of Celtic knots seems to make lots of people assume they symbolize time without end, possibly because they look a bit like the familiar horizontal 8 symbol we use to represent eternity.

Squares: Known as "shield knots" and said to offer protection from evil spirits. They were often placed on battle shields or near sick people.

New or Old Meanings?

We'll never know whether these meanings were really there for the Celts. A key reason the knots are associated with religion is that after the Christians came to power in Ireland, they adapted the knots for their own religious purposes (just as they adopted many Celtic holidays for the Christian calendar). Re-designed versions of the knots appear in Christian scriptures, where intertwined hearts are presented as a Celtic symbol for love. These are usually a good deal more complex than the old Celtic drawings and carvings. Other symbols woven into the knots by Christian calligraphers include crosses, harps, shamrocks and other popular images.

But the knots may not actually come from Ireland. Many scholars believe they were simply brought into Ireland when Norsemen conquered the Celts. Designs that seem similar to the Irish knots have been found in old Italian and British manuscripts, and on pottery and architecture in other parts of Europe. The best historical explanation may be that from the sixth to the eighth centuries, a long series of wars took place between British, Irish, Pictish (Scottish) and Scandinavian tribes, which meant that both winning and loosing groups of warriors wound up living in each other's countries for considerable periods. The influence of all these cultures on each other may be what really gave birth to a style now called Celtic Interlace. A more exotic theory is that Coptic monks from Egypt visited Ireland in the 7th century and brought the design styles with them.

Music of the Celts?

The knots were quite prevalent in the Celtic world, appearing on pottery, buildings and on the familiar Celtic crosses that dot the island. Some of the most beautiful examples turn up on ceremonial jewelry found in archaeological sites in Ireland. Some say the knots are actually a code that makes up a symbolic language, and one intrepid fellow has put forth the idea that they are actually a form of music notation. Few serious historians support either idea.

Whatever their origin, the knots have become favorites of all sorts of "new age" groups, who see them as Celtic love symbols, Celtic symbols of the "Tree of Life" (a concept which had no meaning to the Celts) and a whole range of other things. Wiccans, the modern day pagans who actually follow a number of old Irish traditions, have adopted some very Celtic-looking knot designs as magic symbols. A deeply psychological view of the knots comes from Wikipedia, the popular online encyclopedia, which says "It might even be argued that, from a Jungian point of view of the collective unconscious, the meaning was always there but hidden during the act of creation and revealed in their contemplation." Phew! The most popular interpretation, put forth in countless websites and books, is that because the Celtic knots are almost always "endless" – complete loops without beginnings or end –

they must represent some concept of eternity.

Learning How to Make Them
Happily, you need not be a Wiccan or a psychiatrist to use Celtic knot decorations to add an old Irish flavor to anything from your thumb ring to your living room wall.

If you'd simply like to download some nice pictures of knots to your computer screen, you can find clip art of free Celtic designs, Celtic love symbols and more at http://www.webomator.com/bws/data/rec lip.html

Of course, if you want a good look at some very famous original Celtic knots, pay a visit to the Book of Kells in Dublin, which was created in 800 AD.

11 Shrove Tuesday's Pancake Mania

Shrove Tuesday, the annual pancake feast, takes place each year on the day before Ash Wednesday. This holiday before the start of the Lenten fast, commonly known as "pancake night," is a time when many still engage in the archaic practice of making, tossing and eating mountains of pancakes. Over-indulgence is expected, if not demanded, and children will come into school on Ash Wednesday boasting of their pancake-eating feats. Generally, large, thick pancakes are simply sprinkled with lemon juice and sugar, rolled into a cigar shape and eaten as a sweet.

The survival of this old custom is interesting, since the rigorous Lenten fast is not as widely observed as it once was (though a fair number of people still abstain from alcohol, cigarettes and candy for Lent).

Shrove Tuesday, however, is as popular as ever. The ritual is linked to the great European carnival tradition of Mardi Gras ("Fat Tuesday") when people ate as much fat and meat as possible, knowing that these were forbidden for the next forty days. From the early Middle Ages, the Catholic Church forbade the consumption of meat, eggs and dairy produce

Illustration By Nick Werber

during Lent. On Shrove Tuesday, thrifty housewives made use of the perishable eggs, milk and butter in the preparation of pancakes.

One social aspect of the night, however, has fallen into disuse - the link between Shrove Tuesday and the romantic fortunes of the unmarried. Traditionally in Ireland, marriage was forbidden to take place during Lent, so in the weeks leading up to "Shrovetide," as it's sometimes called, matchmakers busily tried to find suitable candidates for marriage before Ash Wednesday arrived. Households left with unmarried daughters on Shrove Tuesday tried to imbue them with better luck for the coming year by allowing them to toss the first cake. Their pancake-making skills, for better or worse, were seen as an indication of their romantic chances for the next year.

12 Strawboys of the Northwest

If you like unusual headgear, you'll envy the Straw Boys, one of Ireland's most eccentric traditions.

Researching the Straw Boys is a little like studying the Loch Ness Monster. Everyone who writes about them seems to give a different explanation of who they are, where they came from and what they do.

Whenever and wherever they started, the Straw Boys seem to have survived in modern Irish life - at least in the western counties of Ireland where they almost certainly originated. They're most often described as an exceptionally odd bunch of party crashers - young men who appear suddenly at a wedding, possibly uninvited, and dance with the bride and groom before departing as swiftly as they arrived. The only thing that's consistent in all the stories about them is the way they conceal their identities behind stylized hats made of straw.

Still Dancing

Many present-day accounts say that the Straw Boys still appear at weddings from the Achill Island area (northwest county Mayo) on down through the middle west. They're familiar enough, in fact, that some wedding planners offer Straw Boys as a feature you can choose, along with champagne and chocolate cake, from the standard event menu. For about $250, you can apparently have a group of 4-5 of these fellows enter the dinner room, accompanied by a fiddle, dance around the tables for a few minutes, and then lift the bride from her chair and carry her out to the dance floor to begin the "Ceili."

According to Jane Fitzgerald, speaking on a wedding website, "they were boys who rustled cattle. After the job, they'd avoid capture by dressing in straw hats and sneaking into a wedding. They'd drink and dance but never talk. Eventually they got to be a sign of good luck. It's called 'strawing a wedding.'" Another wedding planner advertises Straw Boys who "dance around the bride and groom to protect them from evil spirits." But many traditional accounts say the boys don't appear at the wedding at all, but at the bride's house before the wedding. Still others say that in olden days, weddings were for family members only, and that Straw Boys led friends into the town square to welcome a couple home from their honeymoon.

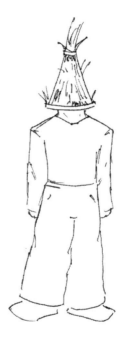

Homeless?

In "The Irish Century," author Michael Morrogh links the Straw Boys to a different tradition, calling them "Irish equivalents of the many groups of mummers who went around acting out traditional plays and songs at Christmas and other times of the year in England. They expected to be rewarded with food and drink in return for the entertainment they offered."

Film buffs may recall a portrayal of 1950's vintage Irish mummers in 1992's "The Playboys," starring Aidan Quinn. The history of traveling performers, says Morrogh, may have arisen out of "a tradition of young, well-educated but homeless men looking for hospitality in return for music and song." A photo in his book portrays a rather jaunty group of Straw Boys, faces concealed by their odd straw hats, visiting an Irish bride before her wedding to play music for her.

Burying the Wren

They seem to be mixed up at times with another group known as the "Wren Boys." These other "boys" go from house to house

on St. Stephen's day (the day after Christmas) singing songs and collecting money to bury a wren, who has died from a collision with the furze, a yellow bramble bush prevalent in the west. They repeat this poem as they go:
"The wren, the wren the king of all birds
St. Steven's day he was caught in the furze
Up with the kettle and down with the pan
Give us some money to bury the wren"

The Wren boys, often around 10 years of age, go about with a decorated holly branch, symbolizing the furze. The money they collect supposedly goes to pay for a "Wren Dance" that evening. It's not really clear whether the Straw Boys are part of this ritual as well, though they're lumped into Christmas celebrations in many books.

If you're in Sligo or Mayo and you happen to come across a Straw Boy, ask him what's the idea of the big hat.

"The Irish Century," by Michael MacCarthy Morrogh. 1998 Robert Rinehard Publisher.

Illustrations by Nick Werber

13 Irish Baby Names

Boy's Names

Aidan ir: Aedan, Aodhan p: "aid+an"
Means "little fire." Often used in remembrance of St. Aidan of Iona, who restored Christianity to Northumbria, England, around 600 AD.

Aindriu or Andrew ir: Aindriu, Aindrias, Andreas p: "ann+drew"
Andrew was one of Christ's 12 apostles. His name was popularized in Ireland by Norman settlers, who brought it there from Scotland. Andrew is that country's patron saint.

Árdal p: "or+dal"
Variant on old Irish name Ardghal, which translates into "high valor." More popular in Northern Ireland than in The Republic.

169

Bram p: "bramm"
Irish for Abraham.

Brendan ir: Breandan, Brandon
p: "bren+dawn"
A large number of saints have this name,
which is translated variously as "prince"
(from original Welsh word "brenhin") or
"little raven." Legend says that the most
famous St. Brendan crossed the Atlantic,
reaching North America, in the 6th century.

Brian p: "bry+enn"
From the Irish word "brigh," which means
"noble and strong." One of the most
popular Irish baby names in Ireland and the
U.S. because of Brian Boru, one of the best
known figures in all of Irish legend. Boru
was a king of Ireland who defeated the
Vikings in 1014 at the Battle of Clontarf,
though he was killed in the battle.

Cathal ir: Cahal p: "ka+hal"
Combination of the Irish words "cath"
which means "battle and "all" which means
"mighty." This name is one of many
variations on "Charles," and has an
association with warriors.

Cian p: "kee+an"
Means "ancient," and is in fact a very old name associated with a son-in-law of King Brian Boru.

Ciaran ir: Kieran, Kieron, Keiran p: "keer-awn"
More than 25 saints have this name, which is fairly common among people of Irish heritage worldwide. Translates into "little dark one."

Cillian ir: Killian p: "kil+e+en"
Cille means "close to the church." St. Cillian went from Ireland to Germany around 650 AD, where he became the Bishop of Wurzburg. He was later executed for forbidding the marriage of a local lord to his brother's widow.

Colm ir: Colum, Columb p: "kul+im"
Translates as "dove." After S. Columba of Iona, a scholar involved in creating the Book of Kells and founding over 40 churches in Ireland around 500 AD.

Connor ir: Connor, Conchobhar p: "con+er"

171

Extremely popular Irish baby name both in Ireland and the U.S. Connected to historical figure Conor McNeasa, who was King Of Ulster. Traslated variously as "strong willed," "desire" and even "lover of hounds." Derives from "con," which means wolf.

Cormac ir: Cormick, Cormack p: "core+mac"
Means "son of charioteer." Eight saints carry this name, as well as an ancient king of Ireland, Cormac Mac Airt, known for wisdom.

Declan ir: Deaglan p: "dek+lan"
Translates into "filled with goodness." St. Declan promoted Christianity in Ireland even before St. Patrick. Several miracles have allegedly taken place on a beach near Ardmore known as "St. Declan's Stone."

Dermot ir: Dermott, Diarmid p: "der+mott"
Old Irish baby name translated variously as "free man" and "free of envy."
Donal ir: Dohhnall, Dumhnuil, Dónall, Domnall p: "doe+naal"

Irish version of either "Donald" or "Daniel," the baby boy name translates as "ruler of the world." This was the name of many old Gaelic kings and noblemen.

Eamon p: "ay+mun"
An English name brought to Ireland by the Normans, probably a variation on "Edmund." Signifies a guardian or protector. One of the more popular Irish baby names in modern times because of Eamon De Valera, the famous President of Ireland from 1959 – 73.

Emmet p: "ehm+et"
Derives from old Saxon name "Amete." Long one of the most widely used baby boy names because of its association with Robert Emmet, a great orator who led the unsuccessful 1798 rebellion against England. Emmet was executed for high treason.

Fergus ir: Fearghus, Fearghais p: "fer+gus"
Translates as "strength" and associated with warriors, but also thought to derive from "fear." Fergus was one of the famous kings of Ulster.

Flann ir: Flan, Flannery p: "flahn"
Translates as "blood red." Many kings,
saints and scholars had this name. A
particularly famous one, Flann Feorna, was
King of Kerry, and is related to the
O'Connor family. It was popular into the
early 20th century, but is today one of the
unusual baby boy names in Ireland.

Gerard ir: Gearoid, Gareth p: "jer+ard"
One of the most common Irish baby names
for boys in Ireland, sometimes shortened to
"Gary." From an old Irish word that
translates as "shining."

Kevin ir: Kevan p: "kev+in"
Derived from old Irish name Coemhghin.
Variously translated as "gentle child" and
"beautiful offspring." St. Kevin founded a
major monastery at Glendalough, County
Wicklow.

Liam ir: Uillium p: "lee+am"
The Irish version of William, which in turn
is originally a German name meaning
"protector."

Malachy p: "ma+la+key"
The Anglicization of many old Irish names
that started with "mael," which means
"servant" or "devotee."

Michael ir: Mychal p: "me+haul"
Popular Irish baby name from the archangel
Michael, who defeated Satan.

Niall ir: Neal, Neil p: "nigh+all"
Name from Northern Ireland that translates
as "chivalry." NIALL (pr. Ni-al), NÉIL (pr.
Nail): From "Neil", "Neale". This is an
Ulster derived name, now used all over
Ireland. Possibly derived from "nel," which
means cloud.

Oisin p: "osh+een"
Son of legendary Irish figures Finn MacCool
and Sive, the goddess. Means "a deer" or
"little deer." A figure who is reputed to have
met St. Patrick, Oisin is the subject of
dozens of Irish legends composed from the
13th century onward.

Patrick ir: Padhraig, Padhraic p: "paud+rik"
From Patrick, the name of Ireland's patron
saint. Perhaps the most popular of all Irish

baby names, it is often cut down to the nickname "Pat" or "Paddy." Translates as "born noble" from the Latin word "patricus." Interestingly, Patrick was never given to children as a name in Ireland before 1700, because it was considered too sacred.

Peadar ir: Peadair p: "peed+ar"
Translates as "the rock." Christ made Peter the leader of his disciples, and he is considered the first Pope.

Quinlan ir: Quilan p: "quin+lin"
Translates as "strong" or "athletic."

Reamonn p: "ray+moon"
Irish for Raymond.

Roibeard ir: Riobard, Robaird p: "ro+baird"
Irish version of the English name Robert, brought to Ireland by the Normans.

Ronan p: "ro+nan"
From the Irish word for "seal." The name is associated with a legend of a seal who becomes trapped in the form of a human (a "selkie" or seal maiden") after violating her

parents' warning never to stray too close to land. She lives a long life as a human but eventually returns to the sea. (A very nice, mysterious treatment of this story is offered in the 1994 movie "The Secret of Roan Inish" by John Sayles.)

Ryan ir: Rhyan, Rian p: "rye+an"
Translates as "little king."

Seamus ir: Seamas, Seumus p: "shay+mas"
Irish for James. Translates as "one who supplants." A shorter version sometimes used is Shimmih, or Jimmy.

Sean ir: Shaun, Shane, Seaghan p: "shawn"
Generally considered the Irish form of John; sometimes defined as another derivation of James. The variation Shane is quite popular in Northern Ireland because of a famous sixteenth century warrior there named Shane O'Neill. Name was brought to Ireland by the Normans. Variously translated as "gift from God" and "God is gracious."

Tomas p: "toe+moss"
Irish form of Thomas. Translates literally as "twin."

Terence ir: Terry, Turlough, Turlach, Terrence p: "ter+rense"
From old Roman name Terrance, which is of unknown translation. Sometimes translated as "tender."

Trevor ir: Treabhar p: "trev+err"
Welsh name translated variously as "prudent" or "great settlement."

Girl's Names

Ailbhe ir: Oilbhe p: "alv+eh"
Said to derive from the English name Olive or from the Irish word for "white" (from Greek word for white "alba.")

Aine ir: Anne p: "awn+ya"
Irish for Ann. Translates as "joy" or "radiance."

Aisling ir: Aislinn, Aislynn, Isleen p: "ash+ling"
Translates as "vision" or "dream" from old Gaelic. One of the more uncommon baby names in Ireland historically, it has become more popular in the 20th century.

Aoife ir: Ava p: "ee+fa"
One of the oldest Irish girls names, derived
from Eva. The name of many characters in
Irish legends, and quite a popular baby name
today in Ireland. Like Ann, translates as
"radient."

Bernadette p: "ber+na+dett"
Saint Bernadette (Bernadette Soubirous) is
famous in Ireland and throughout Europe as
the person the Virgin Mary appeared before
in Lourdes, France, in 1858.

Blath p: "bee+law"
Translates literally from old Irish as "flower"
or "flower bud."

Brigid ir: Brigid, Breedah, Brighdin p:
"bri+heed" or "brid+gett"
A very old and unique baby girl name,
thought to derive from "brigh," the Irish
word for "strength." Name of the daughter
of the fire god in Irish mythology and also
associated with Saint Brighid of Kildare, one
of the patron saints of Ireland. Sometimes
shortened to Bridin or "bride."

Caitriona ir: Catriona, Caitlin, Caiti, Catraoine p: "ca+tree+na"
Irish form of Katherine. Translates as "pure."

Cecilia ir: Cecily, Celia, Cilla, Sisily
p: "si+sill+ya"
From a Roman family name "Caecilius," which means "blind." Brought to Ireland by the Normans.

Ciara ir: Ceara p: "keer+ah"
Translates from old Irish as "black haired one."

Clare ir: Clair, Claire p: "claare"
From a latin word meaning "bright." Name of the western county in Ireland.

Clodagh ir: Clidna, Cliona p: "clo+dah" or "clee+oy+nah"
Old Irish name, whose meaning is not clear. Also the name of a river in County Tipperary.

Deirdre ir: Deedra, Diadra, Diedra
p: "deer+dra"
Translated variously as "sorrowful" and

"fear." A very old but still-popular Irish name. In one Celtic legend, Dierdra was Ireland's most beautiful woman.

Eibhlin ir: Evelyn p: "eye+leen"
Irish form of Eileen. Meaning is unclear.

Eireen p: "eye+reen"
Translates as "peace." The Gaelic form of Irene.

Erin ir: Éirinn p: "air+in"
Translates literally as "Ireland." Used as a girl's given name in modern times.

Fiona p: "fee+nuh"
From Irish word "fion" which means "fair" or "clear." Sometimes lengthened to Fionnuala (p: "fin+oola") meaning "fair shoulders" or "white shoulders." Fionnuala, in turn, is sometimes shortened to Nuala (also pronounced "fin+ooh+la").

Grainne ir: Grace p: "grow+nyuh"
Translates as "grain goddess."

Grania p: "gran+yuh"
Also means "grain goddess." A name most

famous for its association with Grania Mhaol Ni Mhaolmhaigh, the female pirate known to her English enemies as Grace O'Malley. One of the more rare baby names in olden times, it has gained in popularity recently.

Maeve p: "mayve"
Irish form of Meadhbh. Popular in Ireland because of Queen Maeve, a first century B.C. warrior who is one of Ireland's most colorful characters of legend. Her father gave her all of Connaught as a gift. The legendary Queen Maeve, who was possessed of tremendous military and sexual power, is said to be buried in a huge tomb at Knocknarea, in County Sligo.

Maire ir: Mears, Maille, Mariead, Maureen p: "moy+ra"
Irish form of Mary, popular due to the association with the Virgin Mary. Was considered too holy to use as a given name in Ireland up to the 17th century.

Mallaidh p: "mal+ee"
The old Irish form of Molly, a name derived from Mary.

Muireann ir: Murainn p: "moo+eer+en"
Translates from old Irish as "long haired."

Niamh p: "neeve"
Gaelic word meaning "bright."

Patricia ir: Padraigin p: "pa+tri+shuh"
Feminine version of Patrick.

Rioghnach ir: Regina p: "ree+na" or
"ree+oh+na"
Translates as "queen" or "queenly."

Sadhbh ir: Sive, Sally p: "she+veh"
Translates as "goodness."

Sinead ir: Sina, Shinead p: "shin+aid"
Irish for Jane, the feminine version of John.

Siobhan ir: Siubhan p: "shu+vahn"
Irish form of Joan.

Triona p: "tree+nuh"
Shorter version of Catriona, an Irish and
Scottish form of Katherine.

Tara ir: Teamhair p: "ta+ruh"
One of the more unique baby names in
Irish. Was not used as a name through most
of Irish history, only as the name of the
most famous hill of kings in the center of
Ireland. The use of Tara as the estate's name
in "Gone With The Wind," however,
breathed new life into it as a girl's Irish
name.

14 Ireland's Political Structure

Irish Government:
-Type: Republic, parliamentary democracy
- Capital: Dublin
-Administrative divisions (coincide with the 26 counties): Carlow, Cavan, Clare, Cork, Donegal, Dublin, Galway, Kerry, Kildare, Kilkenny, Laois, Leitrim, Limerick, Longford, Louth, Mayo, Meath, Monaghan, Offaly, Roscommon, Sligo, Tipperary, Waterford, Westmeath, Wexford, Wicklow (Note: Cavan, Donegal, and Monaghan are part of the Ulster Province)

Irish independence was granted by treaty with the UK on December 6, 1921

The constitution was first adopted July 1st, 1937 by plebiscite.

The Irish Supreme Court has the right to review all legislative acts.

All citizens 18 years of age can vote.

The head of government is the "Taoiseach" (which literally translates as "chief." Enda Kenny has been Taoiseach since 2011.

Amusing Street Sign, Clare

Ireland has a bicameral parliament called the "Oireachtas," which consists of the Senate and the House.

The Senate ("Seanad Eireann") has 60 seats, 49 of which are elected by the universities

186

from candidates put forward by five vocational panels. Eleven seats are nominated by the Prime Minister. Members serve five-year terms.

The House of Representatives or "Dail Eireann" has 166 seats. Members are elected by popular vote on the basis of proportional representation, and serve five-year terms.

Ireland's flag is comprised of three equal vertical bands of green (hoist side), white, and orange.

To be President of Ireland, one must be at least **35 years of age**.

Irish time is 5 hours ahead of New York Eastern Standard Time.

About The Author

Robert Sullivan grew up in an Irish-German family in the New York area. His close relationship with his maternal grandparents, both of whom were born in Ireland, encouraged him to visit the country in the mid 1970's, when he found it "incredibly backwards but utterly charming." Since then he has returned to Ireland several times, and become more and more interested in all the things that define Irish and Celtic culture. He lives in Port Washington, NY, with his wife and two sons.

He has also complied a book of unique Irish quotations called "Every Goose Thinks His Wife Is A Duck" and operates an Irish culture website at irishletter.com